MENSA®

MATH WIZARD for KIDS

This edition published by Barnes & Noble Inc.,
by arrangement with Carlton Books Limited.

Barnes & Noble Books 1999

Text copyright © British Mensa Limited 1997
Design and artwork copyright © Carlton Books Limited 1997

ISBN 0-7607-1665-X

Printed and bound in Italy

MENSA®

MATH WIZARD for KIDS

JOHN BREMNER

BARNES & NOBLE
BOOKS
NEW YORK

CONTENTS

INTRODUCTION

**Think again if you believe that you cannot do mathematics.
Anyone of average ability can be a Mensa Math Wizard.**

Within this book there are games, puzzles and problems to challenge everyone. Here are all the basics that the average child – or for that matter the average parent – needs to know, presented in a way that makes learning fun. Everybody learns best by doing the things they enjoy.

There are shortcuts here that make math easy. You will discover intriguing patterns to numbers that bring new meaning to what can appear to be a baffling subject. You will kick yourself when you discover how easy some of the things that you thought were impossible really are, and with the aid of a calculator you will discover how to do things in seconds that would have taken Isaac Newton hours to do. You will realize things about moving decimal points, fast multiplying and dividing, finding percentages, rapid mental addition, and using binary numbers.

At the beginning of most new types of puzzle, there is an easy example that allows you to learn the techniques before trying more difficult puzzles. Some you will be able to solve in minutes. Some will keep you entertained for hours. A few are fiendishly difficult, to challenge a budding genius.

The clues given, in most cases, should be enough assistance, if assistance is needed. With younger children, the help of an adult may occasionally be required, but a warning to adults – please do not offer help unless you are asked. When you get help to solve a puzzle, you are less likely to make the effort to do later puzzles too. You should try to set your own level in this book. Puzzles are only fun when we solve them ourselves; when adults get involved, you'll discover that a fun puzzle can all too easily become a homework task.

There is no real structure to the book, with helpful hints, puzzles and games throughout the book. But it is probably best to start with level one puzzles and work your way up to level three. You may even be able to tackle the occasional genius level puzzle. This is because the more puzzles you do, the better you will get at doing them. But, and this is the best part, you improve without having to do the type of boring sets of sums that you find in schoolbooks.

Parts of each puzzle have been specially chosen to give you an idea of math functions that you might never have understood. The great thing about doing math puzzles like these is that you improve your complete math ability. You will learn things here that you will be able to put to use in the real world. The answers are all supplied, with the working too, but try not not to cheat! If you cheat, in the end you only cheat yourself.

There are some problems that you will probably only be able to do with the aid of a calculator so use one if you need to. But remember the golden rule: never use a calculator if you don't need to – except, of course, when you are faced with calculator problems. The aim of the book is for you to use your brain, not the calculator's. If you use a calculator to get the answer, the actual number may be right, but you won't have worked out how you got there and what math principles were used.

In most cases clues have been given only for the easiest examples in a set. The same principles are likely to apply for the rest of the set.

This is a Mensa book. Mensa is an organization where ordinary children and adults who happen to be smart can make contact with other smart people.
For more information on Mensa, contact American Mensa Ltd, 1229 Corporate Drive West, Arlington, TX 76006-6103, USA

Alternatively, if you don't live in the states, contact Mensa International, 15 The Ivories, 628 Northampton Street, London, N1 2NY, UK, who can put you in touch with your own national Mensa.

If you have an internet connection, Mensa can also be found on the World Wide Web at the following addresses, and you will find links to many puzzle sites and related organisations:
American Mensa: http://www.mensa.org/
Mensa Foundation for Gifted Children: http://www.mfgc.org.uk/mfgc/
British Mensa: http://www.mensa.org.uk/mensa/
Australian Mensa: http://www.au.mensa.org/
Mensa Germany:- http://gl15.bio.th-darmstadt.de/mensa/index.html
Mensa Austria : http://gl15.bio.th-darmstadt.de/austria/index_e.htm
Mensa Canada: http://www.canada.mensa.org/francais/int.html
Mensa Finland: http://www.fi.mensa.org/
Mensa France: http://ourworld.compuserve.com/homepages/besnier/m_nmd.htm
Mensa Hungary: http://www.cab.u-szeged.hu/local/mensa/mrend.eng.html
Mensa Belgium-Luxembourg: http://www.mensa.be/

HOW TO DO THE PUZZLES

The following pages will help you to do the puzzles in this section. In a few places, further clues have been supplied. The puzzle numbers in sections 1, 2 and 3 are given after each heading.

Random Numbers
(Puzzle 1)

A random number is one that cannot be predicted. For instance, four random numbers between 1 and 20 are 3, 19, 6 and 8. There is no particular order, even or odd, rising or falling, alphabetic, etc.

Number Search
(Puzzles 2, 3, and 4)

This is an excellent way to boost your numerical reasoning and problem solving. If you work back from the answer, reversing the functions you will come up with the answer. Here is an example:

What number, when you add 3 to it and double the result, gives 48?

48 ÷ 2 (halved, opposite of doubled) **= 24**;
24 – 3 (opposite of + 3) **= 21**. The answer is **21**.
The working for the answer would be **21 + 3 = 24 x 2 = 48.**

Numbagrams
(Puzzles 5, 6, and 7)

A numbagram is just like an anagram, but you rearrange numbers instead of letters. This will help you to boost your understanding of square numbers and square roots. For example 9 x 9 = 81. $9^2 = 81$, 81 is a perfect square and 9 is a square root.

Crossnumber
(Puzzle 8)

This is just like a crossword puzzle, but with numbers instead of words. This should boost your attention span and persistence. You will have a good idea if your answer is close because you may have clue numbers to check against. For example if the down clue is 100 – 12, you may know that the first number is 8 because there is an across clue that is (22 x 40) + 8. The across answer is 888, so you will know the first number of the down clue is 8.

Differences
(Puzzles 9, 10, and 11)

This will improve your number logic. There are other ways of expressing the normal mathematical functions, plus, minus, multiply and divide. For instance there is addition, subtraction, multiplication and division. There is also another way: a sum of numbers means the numbers added together; the difference between numbers is subtraction of (normally) the lower one from the higher one; the product of two numbers would ask you to multiply them and how many times a number is contained in another would be an alternative for division.

Logical sets or Venn Diagrams
(Puzzles 12, 13, and 14)

All mathematical principles work through logic, but sometimes the quantity and complexity of information that we have to organize gets in the way of our logical thinking. If you can't remember what's what, it's hard to be logical. That is where "sets" come in. By organizing similar (or like) items into sets of things, we can easily make sense of confusing amounts of information. Once you know how to do this, you will find many uses for the technique.

For example:

James has 3 birds. Joey can eat square seeds, round seeds and hexagonal seeds. Peggy can eat only hexagonal seeds. Polly can eat hexagonal seeds and round seeds. Can Peggy, Joey, and Polly share a meal?

(Yes / No)

Solution: Yes

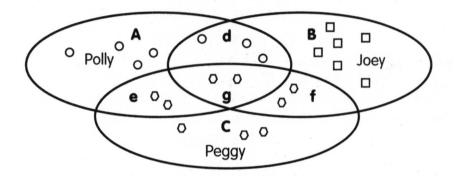

a) Looking at the diagram above it can be seen that there are 3 large circles (called main sets or domains), A, B, and C.

b) d is an intersection of (a shared area that is common to) A and B, but it is not an area that is shared with C.

c) e is common to A and C.

d) f is common to B and C.

e) g is common to all three.

If g contained seeds, for example, you would count them as being in A, B and C.
In mathematical terms, the main sets are A, B and C; the subsets are d, e, f and g.

Looking at the Venn diagram it can be seen that Peggy's only possible food is hexagonal seeds, and that both Joey's and Polly's circles of possibilities include hexagonal seeds. This is the central area with two hexagonal seeds, where Polly, Joey, and Peggy all intersect or unite. They could thus all share a meal of hexagonal seeds. You can also look at the diagram and see that Joey and Polly could share a mixed meal of round and hexagonal seeds. The logic of the information that has been given in the question is seen using the Venn diagram.

PYTHAGORAS

A tribe of Native Americans generally referred to their womenfolk by the animal hide with which they made their blanket. Thus, one woman might be known as Squaw of Buffalo Hide, while another might be known as Squaw of Deer Hide. This tribe had a particularly large and strong woman with a unique animal hide for her blanket. This woman was known as Squaw of Hippopotamus hide, and she was as strong and powerful as the animal from which her blanket was made.

Year after year, this woman entered the tribal wrestling tournament, and easily defeated all challengers; male or female. As the men of the tribe admired her strength and power, this made many of the other woman of the tribe extremely jealous. One year, two of the squaws asked the Chief to allow them to enter their sons together as a wrestling tandem in order to wrestle Squaw of the Hippopotamus hide as a team. In this way, they hoped to see that she would no longer be champion wrestler of the tribe.

As luck would have it, the two sons who were wrestling as a tandem met the squaw in the final and championship round of the wrestling contest. As the match began, it became clear that the squaw had finally met an opponent that was her equal. The two sons wrestled and struggled vigorously and were clearly on an equal footing with the powerful squaw. Their match lasted for hours without a clear victor. Finally the Chief intervened and declared that, in the interests of the health and safety of the wrestlers, the match was to be terminated and that he would declare a winner.

The chief retired to his teepee and contemplated the great struggle he had witnessed, and found it extremely difficult to decide a winner. While the two young men had clearly matched the squaw, he found it difficult to force the squaw to relinquish her tribal championship. After all, it had taken two young men to finally provide her with a decent challenge. No matter how long he thought about it, he couldn't find a solution. Finally. The Chief passed the duty of deciding the winner over to Pythagoras, a visitor from Greece who happened to be staying with the tribe for a while. Pythagoras sat down and thought for a few moments and then his face brightened and he stepped out from the teepee and announced his decision. He said:

"The Squaw of the Hippopotamus is equal to the sons of the squaws of the other two hides!"

If you can remember that punchline perhaps you will remember the theorem of Pythagoras, which states that:

For a right-angled triangle, the square on the hypotenuse is equal to the sum of the squares on the other two sides.

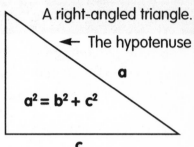

A right-angled triangle.

← The hypotenuse

$a^2 = b^2 + c^2$

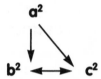

$$a^2 = b^2 + c^2$$
$$b^2 = a^2 - c^2$$
$$c^2 = a^2 - b^2$$

If we know length of two of the sides of any right-angled triangle, we can easily work out the length of the other side.

Example:

Find the length of 'c'. (Don't try measuring any of these to find the solution, as they may not be reproduced to scale. Use Pythagoras' theorem.)

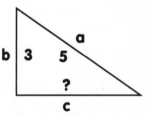

Solution: a = 5 and b = 3, so c = $\sqrt{(5^2 [25] - 3^2 [9])}$ = 16. $\sqrt{16}$ = 4.

Explanation:

Because Pythagoras' theorem works with squares of sides, we have to find the squares (by multiplying the lengths by themselves). Once we know what the squares are we can easily do the adding or subtracting sum before finding the square root of the result.

The above example is actually simpler than it looks because the triangle is in the proportions 3:4:5.

Many builders and carpenters use the 3:4:5 method to check and lay out the right angles of the buildings and projects they are working on. They often make sticks of the right proportions, and nail them together.

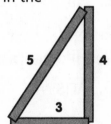

In fact, long before Pythagoras was born in about 580BC, the Egyptians were using the 3:4:5 principle to lay out the pyramids.

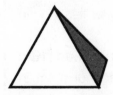

They built pyramids with square bases, and every square pyramid has four right angled triangles. If you don't believe that, try to make one that doesn't!

PERCENTAGES

The term percentage sounds complicated, but percent simply means 100th. So 10% (ten percent) means 10 100ths or $\frac{10}{100}$. Once you realise that percent simply means 100th, all percentages are easy to work out, even if you don't have a calculator.

E.g. Find 13% of 800.

**1% of 800 = $\frac{1}{100}$ of 800 or 800 ÷ 100 = 8,
therefore 13% = 8 x 13 = 104.**

Do a quick check to ensure that the answer is correct.

13% of 800 is the same as 26% of 400
It's easy to figure out that **25% of 400 is 100** (because **25%** is the same as a **quarter**), so we know that our answer is going to be very close at least.

Use a calculator to calculate percentages

E.g. Find 23% of 160.

1. Key in **160**.
2. Hit the multiply (**x** or *****) key.
3. Key in **23**.
4. Hit the percent (**%**).
5. Answer comes up (**36.8**).

DON'T HIT THE EQUALS (=) KEY!

Remember when doing calculations that **of** means the same as **times**. So 23% of 160 means 160 x 23%

Tips for getting the right answer

- Be careful to press the correct buttons when keying in.
- Don't automatically believe the calculator until you see that the answer ties in with common sense.
- It is easy to accidentally press an extra number, or to put the decimal point in the wrong place

STARTER LEVEL PUZZLES

Puzzle 1

Draw a straight line to divide this square into two halves, with a total of 15 in each half.

```
        3       1
            2       3
   6
   4           2
        1
   3           4   1
```

Puzzle 2

Circle the shape with most sides.

Puzzle 3

Circle the fraction that is closest to 1.

$$\frac{1}{2} \quad \frac{3}{4} \quad \frac{1}{8} \quad \frac{1}{3} \quad \frac{2}{3}$$

Puzzle 4

Circle the smallest fraction.

$$\frac{1}{4} \quad \frac{2}{9} \quad \frac{1}{3} \quad \frac{2}{7} \quad \frac{5}{6}$$

✔ *Turn to page 19 for the answers*

Puzzle 5

Circle the two numbers that are not even numbers.

12 4 16 5 6 2 7 20 8

Puzzle 6

Circle the sphere and the cube.

Puzzle 7

What is there more of here, fleas or bees?

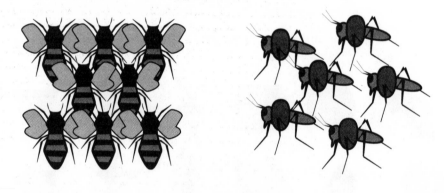

Puzzle 8

What has most legs, two spiders and a horse, or nine eagles?

✔ *Turn to page 19 for the answers*

Puzzle 9

Which archer scored more, Fraser or Lorna? You can see the holes left when the arrows were pulled out.

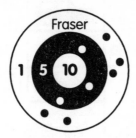

Puzzle 10

Which of these shapes has right angles in it? (Right angles are 90° angles.)

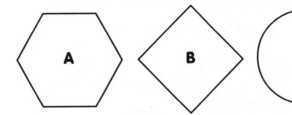

Puzzle 11

Which of these numbers can be divided evenly by 3, but not by 2?

18 15 12 6

Puzzle 12

Which team is likely to win at tug-of-war, team A or team B? Every person on each team is the same weight and strength.

A   B

✔ *Turn to page 19 for the answers*

Puzzle 13

How many white cars with black windows are in this multi-storey car park?

Puzzle 14

If you divided the number of leaves on this rose by 2.5, how many would you have?

Puzzle 15

How many different types of symbol are used in this message from the Aztecs? Each symbol is made up from a number of different shapes.

✔ **Turn to page 19 for the answers**

Puzzle 16

How many bubbles has this frogman blown?

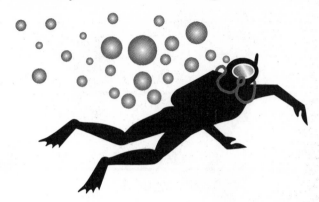

Puzzle 17

How many times does the smaller cog turn for every three complete rotations that the bigger cog makes?

Puzzle 18

Which balanced ball is most likely to fall off?

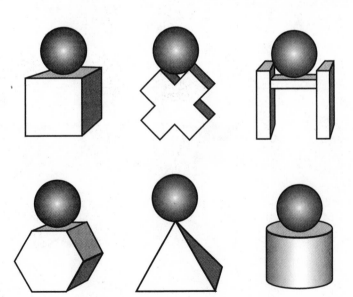

✔ *Turn to pages 19 – 20 for answers*

Puzzle 19

How many white stars are in this collection?

✔ *Turn to page 20 for the answers*

STARTERS ANSWERS

1.

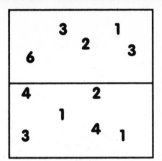

2.

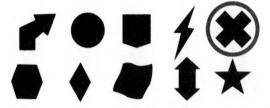

3.
$\dfrac{3}{4}$

4.
$\dfrac{2}{9}$

5.
5 and 7.

6.

7.
Bees. There are eight bees, but only six fleas.

8.
Two Spiders (eight legs each) + 1 horse (four legs) have more legs (8 + 8 + 4 = 20) than nine eagles (2 legs each; 9 x 2 =18).

9.
Lorna. Lorna has scored 22, but Fraser has scored only 20.

10.
Shape B, the square. Every square has four 90° angles in it, even if the square is tilted onto a corner.

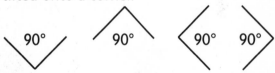

11.
15. 15 ÷ 2 = 7½.

12.
Team B. Because each person has the same strength and weight, the team with most members will win.

13.
8 cars with black windows.

14.
2.4. There are 6 petals, so 6 ÷ 2.5 = 2.4.

15.
5. Each symbol in the top row is used once in each row.

STARTERS ANSWERS

16.
24 bubbles.

17.
6 complete rotations. The large cog has 16 teeth and the small one has 8. As the large cog has turned three full circles, the number of teeth rotated is 48 (16 x 3). The small wheel must also have rotated 48 cogs, so 48 ÷ 8 = 6.

18.
The one on the pyramid.

19.
150.

PUZZLES LEVEL 1

Puzzle 1 (Random Number Squares)

Draw two straight lines to make a smaller square inside this big square, with a total of 25 in the small square. Remember that a square has 4 equal sides.

```
2        7        1              0
 0           6          0
     5            8
                1           4
   2       9        0    5
 2
     0        7        4
                         6
 9      6        2
           0              6
```

Clue:

Don't add the zeros!

Puzzle 2 (Number Search)

What number, when you add 7 to it, multiply that by 3, and take away 40, gives you 173?

Clue:

Work backwards. For example, using the example provided on page 7,
$48 \div 2 = 24$; $24 - 3 = 21$.

Puzzle 3 (Number Search)

What number, when you take 4 from it and multiply the result by two, gives you 64?

Puzzle 4 (Number Search)

What number, when you take 6 from it, divide the result by 2, and divide the result of that by 8, gives you 4?

Puzzle 5 (Numbagrams)

Rearrange the digits to get two perfect squares. **526**   [_ _ _]   [_ _ _]

Clue:

When you find the square root of a number you will know if that number is a perfect square. Non-perfect squares will have square roots that are not whole numbers. Tip: A perfect square is the result of multiplying a number by itself and getting a whole number answer. Example: $9 \times 9 = 81$, so 81 is a perfect square and 9 is the square root of 81.

✓ **Turn to page 26 for the answers**

Puzzle 6 (Numbagrams)

Rearrange the digits to get a perfect square. **892** [_ _ _]

Puzzle 7 (Numbagrams)

Rearrange the digits to get a perfect square. **2140** [_ _ _ _]

Puzzle 8 (Crossnumber)

Put the numbers in the blank squares.

Across

1. 11 x 12
5. Knock the last zero from 400 x 400, and add 10
7. 512 ÷ 2
10. 1 less than a five-digit number

Down

1. √121
2. 56789 – 20730
3. √400
4. 360 ÷ 4
6. Double the square of 3
8. 23 x 3
9. An odd number just less than 20

Tip: Solve the down clues first.

Puzzle 9 (Differences)

When you add two numbers their total is 15. When you compare the numbers their difference is 3. What are the two numbers?

Clue:

Look at the possibilities. For example, you can tell that the solution is not 12 and 3, because the difference between 12 and 3 is 9.

✔ *Turn to page 26 for the answers*

Puzzle 10 (Differences)

When you add two numbers their total is 29. When you compare them their difference is 5. What are the two numbers?

Puzzle 11 (Differences)

When you add two numbers their total is 43. When you compare them their difference is 9. What are the two numbers?

Puzzle 12 (Venn Diagrams)

Ben, Zeke and Marsha all live in overlapping plots of woodland. They share the cost of the upkeep of some trees. Look at the diagram below and decide the following:

a) How many trees do only Marsha and Zeke share the upkeep of?
b) How many trees do only Marsha and Ben share the upkeep of?
c) How many trees do only Ben and Zeke share the upkeep of?
d) How many trees do Marsha, Zeke, and Ben share the upkeep of?

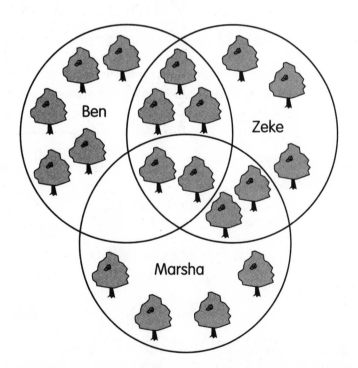

✔ *Turn to page 26 for the answers*

Puzzle 13 (Venn Diagrams)

In Cyclopopolis there are three overlapping cycling zones, imaginatively named, Zone 1, Zone 2, and Zone 3. They are all environmentally conscious, and share the cost of maintaining some of the free bicycles which the residents use. With that in mind, referring to the Venn diagram below, answer the following:

a) How many bicycles do Zone 1 and Zone 2 share the cost of maintaining?

b) How many bicycles do Zone 2 and Zone 3 share the cost of maintaining?

c) How many bicycles do Zone 1 and Zone 3 share the cost of maintaining?

d) How many bicycles do Zone 1, Zone 2 and Zone 3 equally share the cost of maintaining?

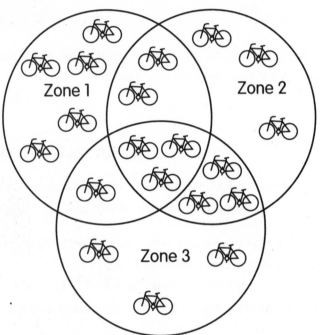

Puzzle 14 (Venn Diagrams)

Biff, Rover and Hilda, three puppies, all share the same house. Their fleas all share the same house too, and, being social animals, they sometimes share the same host. With that in mind, referring to the Venn diagram below, answer the following:

a) How many fleas does Rover only share with Hilda?

b) How many fleas does Biff only share with Hilda?

c) How many fleas does Rover only share with Biff?

d) How many fleas does Biff share with both Rover and Hilda?

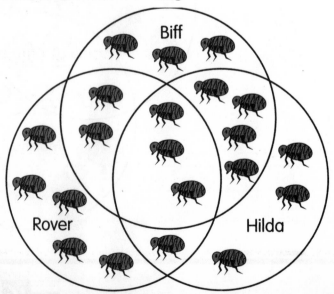

 Turn to page 26 for the answers

24

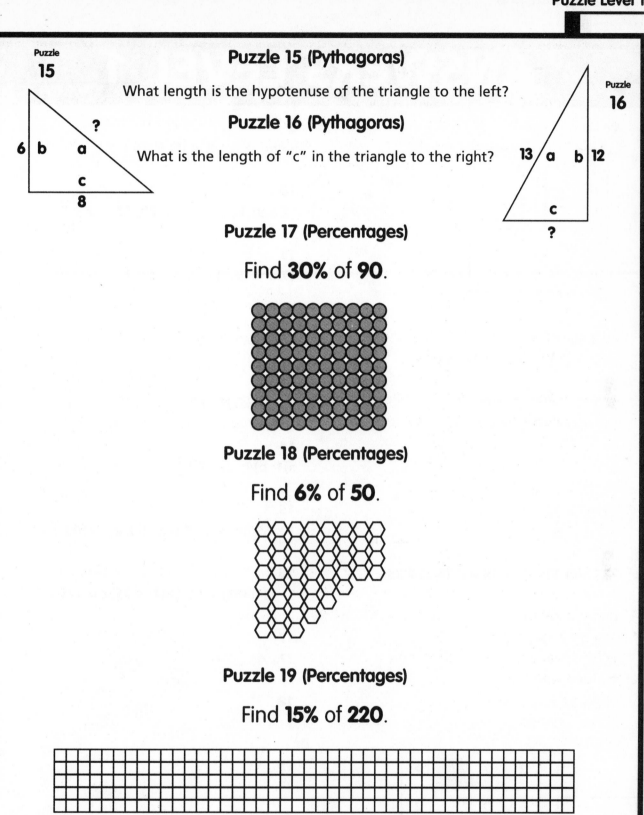

Puzzle 15 (Pythagoras)

What length is the hypotenuse of the triangle to the left?

Puzzle 16 (Pythagoras)

What is the length of "c" in the triangle to the right?

Puzzle 17 (Percentages)

Find **30%** of **90**.

Puzzle 18 (Percentages)

Find **6%** of **50**.

Puzzle 19 (Percentages)

Find **15%** of **220**.

✔ *Turn to page 26 for the answers*

ANSWERS LEVEL 1

1

2

64. 64 + 7 = 71;
71 x 3 = 213; 213 – 40 = 173.

3

36. 36 – 4 = 32; 32 x 2 = 64.

4

70. 70 – 6 = 64;
64 ÷ 2 = 32; 32 ÷ 8 = 4.

5

256 and 625. 16 x 16 = 256; 25 x 25 = 625.

6

289. 17 x 17 = 289.

7

1024. 32 x 32 = 1024.

8

9

6 and 9. 6 + 9 = 15; 9 – 6 = 3.

10

12 and 17. 12 + 17 = 29; 17 – 12 = 5.

11

17 and 26. 17 + 26 = 43; 26 – 17 = 9.

12

a)2; b)0; c)3; d)2.

13

a)2; b)3; c)1; d)3.

14

a)1; b)4; c)2; d)3.

15

10. 6^2 (36) + 8^2 (64) = 100. a = $\sqrt{100}$ = 10.

16

5. 13^2 (169) – 12^2 (144) = 25. c = $\sqrt{25}$ = 5.

17

27.

18

3.

19

33.

PUZZLES LEVEL 2

Puzzle 1 (Random Number Squares)

Draw a smaller square, this time a diamond shape, inside this big square, with a total of 55 in the small square.

```
2                       0
      7        1
0          6        0
     5         8
             1        4
      2    9    0    5
  2
       0         4
            7        6
   9      6      2
             0          6
```

Clue:

The smaller square, in this case, sits diagonally inside the bigger square.

Puzzle 2 (Number Search)

What number, when you multiply it by 4 and subtract 19.5 from the result, gives you a number that when added to itself will give 5 as a result if subtracted from the value that is double the value of 12 squared?

Puzzle 3 (Number Search)

What number, when you multiply it by 16, gives you a number that, when its square root is subtracted from it, gives 132?

Puzzle 4 (Number Search)

What number, when 1.2 is added to it, gives a number that, when divided by 10, produces the same result as finding the square root of 9?

Tip:

A palindromic number is a number that reads the same backwards and forwards, such as 22, 454, or 67776.

Puzzle 5 (Numbagrams)

Rearrange the digits to get a perfect square + 5. **347 [_ _ _]**

✔ *Turn to page 32 for the answers*

27

Puzzle 6 (Numbagrams)

Rearrange the digits to get a perfect square + 1. The first digit is not a zero (0).

8002 [_ _ _ _]

Puzzle 7 (Numbagrams)

Rearrange the digits to get a perfect square + 4. **1403** [_ _ _ _]

Puzzle 8 (Crossnumber)

Put the numbers in the blank squares. Some answers may start with zero (0).

1	2		3	4		5	6
7		8			9		
10				11			
		12					
	13			14		15	
16			17		18		19
20				21			
22			23			24	

Tip:

Do working in brackets first, when calculating.

✓ *Turn to page 32 for the answers*

Across

1. The largest possible sum of 2 squares to equal less than 90

3. *22 across* + 66

5. $\sqrt{361}$

7. Consecutive sequence of digits 39 + 10 + 10 + 10

10. 1545 reduced by a factor of 3

11. 455 x 8

12. $\sqrt{2025}$

13. One-fifteenth of 225

14. Double what *17 down* would be with the 2nd and 3rd digits reversed

16. One-quarter of 8172

18. *5 down* – 18

20. A palindromic number that starts with 1158

22. Any number multiplied by zero

23. $\sqrt{4624}$

24. (11 x 10) – (11 x 2)

Down

1. 9000 – 644

2. 30^2 + 91

3. (8 x 9) – 3

4. 1000 – 347

5. 41 x 4

6. 10000 – 92

8. *12 across* repeated

9. 192463 x 5

13. Could be binary

15. The first 2 digits are 8^2; the second 2 digits are $\sqrt{324}$

16. 17.5 x 12

17. 20^2 – 14

19. 30^2 + double the first digit of the result – 300

21. Perfectly divided by 11 or 8

Puzzle 9 (Differences)

When you add two numbers their total is 180. When you compare the numbers their difference is 68. What are the two numbers?

Puzzle 10 (Differences)

When you add two numbers their total is 138. When you compare them their difference is 90. What are the two numbers?

Puzzle 11 (Differences)

When you add two numbers their total is 102. When you compare them their difference is 28. What are the two numbers?

✔ *Turn to page 32 for the answers*

Puzzle 12 (Venn Diagrams)

Fiona, Mary, and Anee all collect shoes which fit themselves. Fiona has 14 pairs. Anee has 7 pairs. Mary has 10 pairs. Three of Anee's pairs fit Fiona. Six of Fiona's pairs fit Anee. Two of Mary's pairs fit Fiona but not Anee, two of Mary's pairs fit Anee but not Fiona, and three of Mary's pairs fit both Anee and Fiona. How many pairs fit all three girls? Use the different shapes to the right to represent shoes in the Venn diagram.

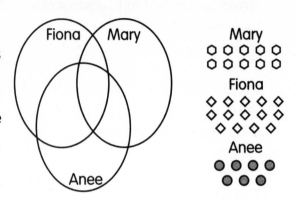

Puzzle 13 (Venn Diagrams)

In a race of fourteen strange rabbits, in which all of them ran, two of the rabbits also hopped; six of the rabbits also skipped, and two of the rabbits also rolled. But one who rolled was one who also skipped, and two who hopped were from the group who also skipped. The remainder just ran. How many ran and skipped, but didn't hop or roll?

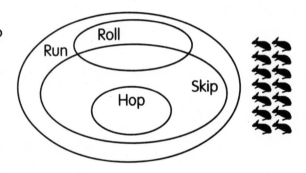

Puzzle 14 (Venn Diagrams)

There are 22 penguins in a scattered colony. When not out fishing, five of them stay on the rocks; four of them stay on the shore, and four on the cliff. Three penguins are happy to stay on either the cliff or the shore; two are happy to go on the rocks or the shore; one penguin has a preference for either the rocks or the cliff; and three penguins split their time between rocks, cliff, and shore. Draw the penguins in the appropriate place on the Venn Diagram to the right.

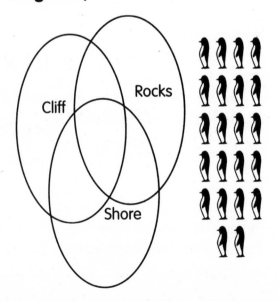

✓ *Turn to page 33 for the answers*

Puzzle 15 (Pythagoras)

What length is the diagonal across this square? (Round to 2 decimal places.)

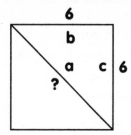

Puzzle 16 (Pythagoras)

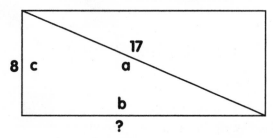

What is the length of "b" in this square?

Puzzle 17 (Percentages)

What percentage of 180 is 12?

Puzzle 18 (Percentages)

In a parking lot of 97 cars, a parking warden calculated that 97% of the cars in the lot, on average, were overstaying their parking permit. To the nearest whole car, how many would that be?

Puzzle 19 (Percentages)

In a land of giants, a large drinking glass that held 192 pints was only 17% full. How much more cola was needed to fill the glass?

✔ Turn to page 33 for the answers

ANSWERS LEVEL 2

1

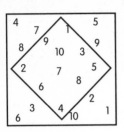

2

40. 40 x 4 = 160;
160 – 19.5 = 141.5;
141.5 + 141.5 = 283;
288 – 283 = 5.

3

9. 9 x 16 = 144;
144 – 12 = 132.

4

28.8. 28.8 + 1.2 = 30;
30 ÷ 10 = 3; √9 = 3.

5

734. 729 + 5;
729 = 27 x 27.

6

2080. 2079 + 1;
2079 = 63 x 63.

7

3140. 3136 + 4;
3136 = 56 x 56.

8

¹8	²9		³6	⁴6		⁵1	⁶9
⁷3	9	⁸4	9	5	⁹9	6	9
¹⁰5	1	5		¹¹3	6	4	0
6		¹²4	5		2		8
	¹³1	5		¹⁴7	3	¹⁵6	
¹⁶2	0	4	¹⁷3		¹⁸1	4	¹⁹6
²⁰1	1	5	8	²¹8	5	1	1
²²0	0		²³6	8		²⁴8	8

9

56 and 124. 56 + 124 = 180;
124 – 56 = 68.

10

24 and 114. 24 + 114 = 138;
114 – 24 = 90.

11

37 and 65. 37 + 65 = 102;
65 – 37 = 28.

ANSWERS LEVEL 2

12

3 pairs.

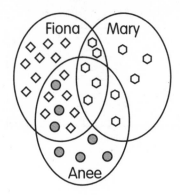

13

3.

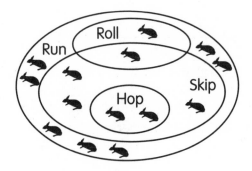

14

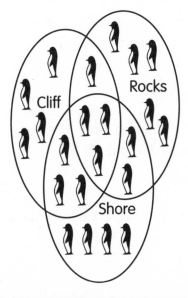

15

8.49. 6^2 (36) + 6^2 (36) = 72. $\sqrt{72}$ = 8.49.

16

15. 17^2 (289) − 8^2 (64) = 225. $\sqrt{225}$ = 15.

17

6.67%. 12 ÷ 180 = 0.06666r; x 100 = 6.666.

18

94. 97 x 97 = 9409;

9409 ÷ 100 = 94.09%; 94 is the nearest whole number to 94.09.

19

159.36 pints. 192 x 17% = 32.64;

192 − 32.64 = 159.36.

PUZZLES LEVEL 3

Puzzle 1 (Random Number squares)

Draw two straight lines inside this square to divide it into four sections. The sum of numbers in each section will be 60. Both lines will go from one edge of the square to another.

Clue:

The two lines cross at the point marked with the black spot.

```
9 2   1   2    3  7      1        8
7   1     7  1       5    1
        2     7 9   3       3   1
5                  2
     2   5  4   3   2      4
              3        1     8
     2   1    9   7  7
                  2            1
7   4                    1   6
                             1
9     3     9         7
              3
       1          1         9
5          7
     3              3      2
2         2            1
```

Puzzle 2 (Number search)

What four-digit number, all prime digits, has 19 as a factor for its last two digits, when subtracted from its reverse produces 6174, and when added to its reverse produces a palindromic number less than 9999?

Puzzle 3 (Number search)

What is the four-digit number, which when you add its digits gives you 15; if its reverse is subtracted from 9669 produces itself; and which has digits progressively smaller from left to right, with the right hand digit being four times smaller than the digit that is 2nd from the left?

Puzzle 4 (Number search)

What two factors of 7950, when added together produce 203 and when the larger factor is divided by the smaller factor produce a number between 2.5 and 3?

Puzzle 5 (Numbagrams)

Rearrange the digits to give a number that is the total of two perfect squares added, one of which has a square root that is half the value of the other:

8210 [_ _ _ _]

✔ *Turn to page 40 for the answers*

Puzzle 6 (Numbagrams)

Rearrange the digits to give a number that is the total of two perfect squares multiplied together:

5522 [_ _ _ _]

Puzzle 7 (Numbagrams)

Rearrange the digits to give a number that is two perfect squares next to each other, with the lower on the left, with one of the square roots being a greater value less than 100 than the other is greater than 1:

2517296 [_ _ _ _ _ _ _]

Puzzle 8 (Crossnumber)

Put the numbers in the blank squares. Some answers may start with a 0 (zero).

Across

1. 356 in binary
9. $\sqrt{8352100}$
10. *24 across* + 567
11. 60^2
12. *25 across* + 240
13. Repetition of 8 x 9
14. *22 across* – 2075
15. $73^2 + \sqrt{1369}$
19. *19 down* – 125
22. $\sqrt{99980001}$
23. Second two digits – first two digits = 54, which is double the first two digits
24. 404 x 11
25. Double *2 across* + (36 x 10)
26. 1828613.5 x 8 to the power of 3 (8 x 8 x 8 or 8^3)

Down

1. 866361643 ÷ 7
2. Less than 1000. The last two digits total the first significant digit
3. *20 down* + 196
4. 2 more than the number of metres in a kilometre
5. 63 x 9
6. 1038 greater than 1
7. $\sqrt{33124}$
8. 5232551 x 2
16. This number, plus itself, gives 7886
17. *18 down* + 4
18. (6 x *6 down*) + 708
19. 100 x 22.6
20. 2 two-digit prime numbers put together which, if added, total 28
21. The first two digits from the last two digits is 3. The sum of all digits is 16

Turn to page 40 for the answers

Puzzle 9 (Differences)

When you add two square roots their total is 14. When you compare their squares the difference is 28. What are the two square roots?

Puzzle 10 (Differences)

When you add two square roots their total is 24. When you compare their squares the difference is 144. What are the two square roots?

Puzzle 11 (Differences)

When you add two square roots their total is 19. When you compare their squares the difference is 133. What are the two square roots?

Puzzle 12 (Venn Diagrams)

Roy, Joe, Ann and Pat own orchards with overlapping borders. They share fallen apples when they lie on common ground. Referring to the Venn diagram below, how many apples are on the common ground of:

a) Ann and Pat only?

b) Ann and Joe only?

c) Joe and Roy only?

d) Roy, Pat, and Joe only?

e) All four people only?

f) Ann, Pat, and Joe only?

g) Ann, Roy, and Joe only?

h) Ann, Pat, and Roy only?

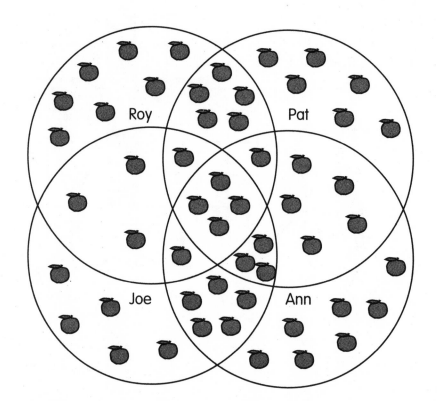

✔ *Turn to page 41 for the answers*

Puzzle 13 (Venn Diagrams)

In Lingolingoland, a mathematician owns the language and everyone must pay taxes to her according to how many similes, suggestions, analogies, and paradigms they use. In all, 33 people use suggestions; 28 use similes; 28 use paradigms and 31 use analogies. But there are only 67 people in Lingolingoland, so some use more than one of the taxable language elements. Six people use paradigms alone, seven only similes, nine just suggestions, and eight just analogies. Two use everything except similes, while five use similes and paradigms but nothing else. Seven use analogies and suggestions but not paradigms or similes. Show how this is possible using the Venn diagram below, and figure out:

a) How many use both analogies and paradigms but not similes or suggestions?
b) How many use paradigms, similes, and suggestions, but not analogies?
c) How many use analogies, paradigms and similes, but not suggestions?
d) How many use similes, suggestions and analogies, but not paradigms?
e) How many use paradigms, similes, suggestions and analogies?

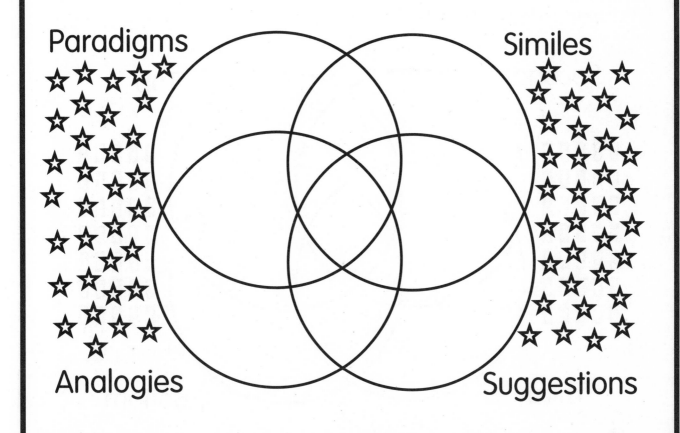

✔ **Turn to page 41 for the answers**

Puzzle 14 (Venn Diagrams)

Pia has four bookshelves. She has 70 different books, among which are a number of duplicates. On the top bookshelf she has 36 books. On the second bookshelf there are 30 books. On her third bookshelf there are 31 books. On her bottom bookshelf she has 31 books. 10 books are only found on the top shelf, six are only found on the second shelf, 8 are only found on the third shelf, and 6 are only found on the bottom shelf. Five books are on the top and second shelves only, while six are only on both the third and bottom shelves. Show how this is possible using the Venn diagram below, and answer the following.

a) How many books are common to the third and the second bookshelves?
b) How many books are common to the top and the bottom bookshelves?
c) How many books do the top and the third bookshelves have in common, that no others have in common?
d) How many books are common to the top, second and bottom shelves, but not on the third shelf?
e) How many books are on the top, third and bottom shelves, but not on the second shelf?
f) How many books are common to all four shelves?

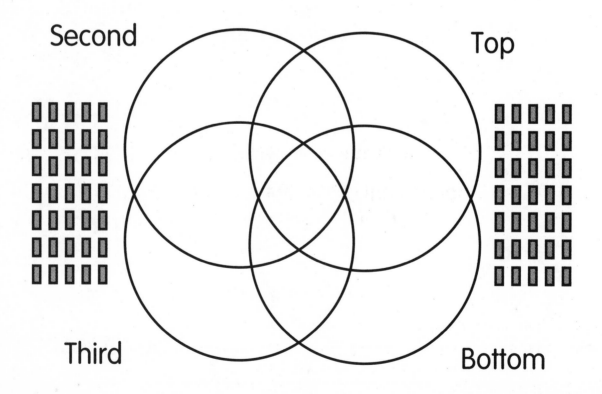

Turn to page 41 for the answers

Puzzle 15 (Pythagoras)

Find the missing value. (Round to 2 decimal places.)

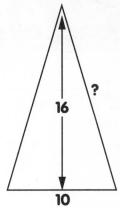

Puzzle 16 (Pythagoras)

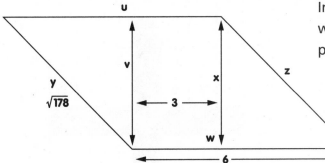

In this parallelogram, find the value of "x", when u and w, v and x, and y and z are parallel; and the angle of u and x is 90°.

Puzzle 17 (Percentages)

What percent of **243** is **3.3%** of **26**?

Puzzle 18 (Percentages)

What percent of **194.194** is **21.6%** of **21.6**?

(Round to 2 decimal places)

Puzzle 19 (Percentages)

A space craft holding 6.666666 million litres of fuel, which can travel at 666666 kilometres per second, uses 16% of its fuel every minute of full thrust. How long can it stay at full thrust?

✔ *Turn to page 41 for the answers*

ANSWERS LEVEL 3

1

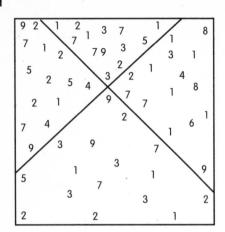

2

1357. 19 is a factor of 57 (x 3), 7531 –
1357 = 6174;
1357 + 7531 = 8888.

3

8421. 8 + 4 + 2 + 1 = 15;
9669 – 1247 = 8421;
4 (second digit from left) is four times
larger than 1 (right digit).

4

53 and 150. 53 x 150 = 7950;
53 + 150 = 203;
150 ÷ 53 = 2.83

5

1280. (32 x 32) [1024] + (16 x 16) [256] =
1280.

6.

2525.
(50 x 50) [2500] + (5 x 5) [25] = 2525.

7

1967225. 14 x 14 = 196;
85 x 85 = 7225;
100 – 85 = 15;
15 is greater than 14 – 1 (13).

8

¹1	²0	³1	⁴1	0	⁵0	⁶1	⁷0	⁸0
⁹2	8	9	0			¹⁰5	0	1	1
¹¹3	6	0	0		¹²6	3	8	0
¹³7	2	7	2		¹⁴7	9	2	4
6								6
¹⁵5	¹⁶3	¹⁷6	¹⁸6		¹⁹2	²⁰1	²¹3	5
²²9	9	9	9		²³2	7	8	1
²⁴4	4	4	4		²⁶6	1	4	0
9	3	6	2	5	0	1	1	2

9

6 and 8. 6 + 8 = 14;
6 x 6 = 36;
8 x 8 = 64;
64 – 36 = 28.

10

9 and 15. 9 + 15 = 24;
9 x 9 = 81; 15 x 15 = 225;
225 – 81 = 144.

11

6 and 13. 6 x 6 = 36;
13 x 13 = 169;
169 – 36 = 133.

ANSWERS LEVEL 3

12
a) 5.
b) 5.
c) 3.
d) 1.
e) 4.
f) 3.
g) 1.
h) 1.

13
a) 7.
b) 3.
c) 1.
d) 2.
e) 4.

14
a) 16.
b) 18.
c) 0.
d) 3.
e) 1.
f) 6.

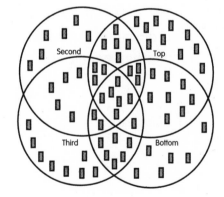

15.
16.76. Since the base is 10, use half the base to make the equivalent of a right-angled triangle.
16^2 (256) + 5^2 (25) = 281. $\sqrt{281}$ = 16.76.

16.
13. This is a parallelogram, therefore y = z ($\sqrt{178}$). The distance between v and x is 3, and u and w is 6. Thus the size of the triangle must be z, x and ½w. The hypotenuse is z ($\sqrt{178}$) – ½w [3^2] (9) = 169; $\sqrt{169}$ = 13.

17
0.35%. 3.3% of 26 = 0.858;
0.858 ÷ 243 = 0.0035304; if the answer was 0.01, it would be 1%, so 0.0035 = 0.35%.

18
2.40%. 21.6 x 21.6% = 4.6656;
4.6656 ÷ 194.194 = 0.0240; 0.0240 x 100 = 2.40%.

19
6.25 minutes (6 minutes and 15 seconds).
100 ÷ 16 = 6.25.

GENIUS LEVEL 4

Puzzle 1

Draw four straight lines that divide this puzzle into eight parts, with a total of 25, 26, 27, 28, 29, 30, 31, and 32 each having one part. At least one end of each line touches the edge of the rectangle.

```
2  6   7   1    2      8  0  5 1 3 9 0 1
  1  3 7     0    1  0      3  9  3    7      7
7                                     0  1
   0     1 7 0 7       0 9  9 3        0     3
  4     2               8      1  5     0  3
0      0 7  0    4        2   1     2
  1   0    5  0          0    4    0
5   2              3      1  0 3  1    6  0   7
2  9  1   1  3  0    1  2  0  9              1
```

Puzzle 2

What five-digit palindromic number, if subtracted from a palindromic number that has every digit equal to the sum of either the first three digits of the original palindromic number added together, or the sum of the last three digits of the original palindromic number added together, produces a result that, if all the digits are added together equals 21; or if it is subtracted from a sum that has all the digits equal to the result of the 2nd and 3rd digits or the 3rd and 4th digits of the original palindromic number added together, produces a result that, if all the digits are added together, equals 16?

Puzzle 3

Rearrange **503402726** to get a perfect square +1, which has a square root less than 26000 and more than 25000:

[_ _ _ _ _ _ _ _ _]

Puzzle 4

When you add three square roots their total is 41. When you compare the difference between the total of the squares of the first two square roots with the total of the squares of the second two square roots, the result is 203. What are the three square roots?

✔ **Turn to page 44 for the answers**

Puzzle 5

Obadiah Wisdomtooth is a good dentist, but a poor organiser. He has 100 false teeth, of various classifications. Because every tooth is different, some of them may be classified in more than one group, and Obadiah gets confused. He can classify 45 teeth in group 1; 39 in group 2; 72 in group 3; 40 in group 4, and 37 in group 5.

Eight teeth are common to groups 1 and 3, but no other group; and seven teeth are common to groups 3 and 5, but no other group. There are six teeth in group 2 that are in no other group, six teeth in group 3 that are in no other group, seven teeth in group 4 that are in no other group, and there are seven teeth in group 5 that are in no other group. One tooth is only in groups 1 and 2, and six more are in group 3 as well. There are 3 teeth in groups 3 and 4 only, and four in groups 3, 4 and 5. Nine teeth are in 2, 3 and 5.

Show how this is possible using the Venn diagram below, and answer the following:

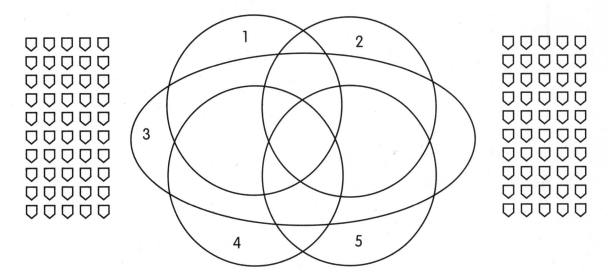

a) How many teeth are common to groups 4 and 5, but not to any other group?

b) How many teeth are common to groups 2 and 5, but not to any other group?

c) How many teeth are in group 1 and not in any other group?

d) How many teeth are common to groups 1, 3 and 4, but not to any other group?

e) How many teeth are common to all groups?

f) How many teeth are common to all groups except group 5?

g) How many teeth are common to all groups except group 4?

 Turn to page 44 for the answers

ANSWERS – GENIUS LEVEL

1

2

12321. 66666 − 12321 = 54345;

5 + 4 + 3 + 4 + 5 = 21;

55555 − 12321 = 43234;

4 + 3 + 2 + 3 + 4 = 16.

3

627402305. 627402305 − 1 = 627402304;

25048 x 25048 = 627402304.

4

11, 12 and 18. 11 + 12 + 18 = 41;

11 x 11 = 121;

12 x 12 = 144;

18 x 18 = 324;

324 + 144 = 468;

121 + 144 = 265;

468 − 265 = 203.

5

a) 1.

b) 0.

c) 6.

d) 14.

e) 6.

f) 1.

g) 2.

ABOUT CALCULATORS

You will need a calculator to be able to do some of the games and puzzles in this book.

Any pocket calculator will do, if it has a square root function. If you have a personal computer, the chances are that it will have a calculator programme too. Some of these computer calculators can actually be changed into a full scientific calculator. The functions shown below are the same as those that are available on a non-scientific calculator, and this is all that is required for most of the puzzles in this book.

The best way to get to know a calculator is to use it.
Try out all the functions. You cannot harm a calculator by pressing the buttons.

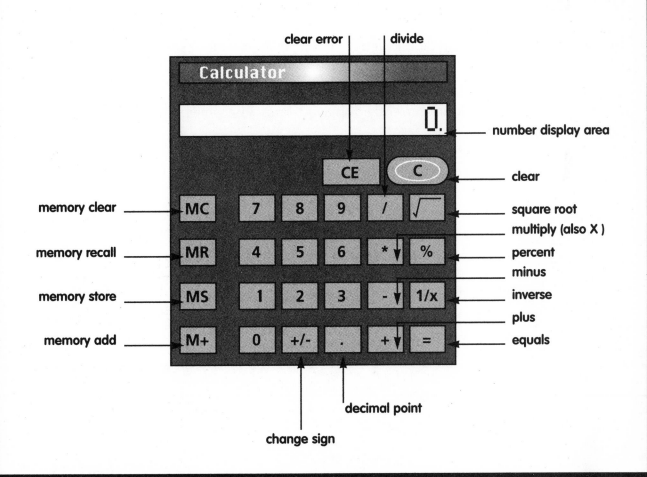

45

Functions

Most functions are self-explanatory. The square root key will find the square root of the figure currently displayed. The multiply key will multiply, etc.

Memory store:

Puts the current figure in the number display area into memory.

Memory add:

Adds the currently displayed figure to the number already stored in memory.

Clear error:

Clears away the last number keyed in, without removing the rest of the calculation that you have been working on.

Back:

Wipes out the last individual digit keyed in. Thus 23456 becomes 2345.

Inverse:

Finds the inverse of the figure currently displayed. Thus 3 becomes $\frac{1}{3}$ = 0.333333333r.

Change sign:

Changes a positive figure such as 35 into the equivalent minus figure, in this case –35.

Scientific Calculator

Additional functions are here for advanced mathematical and statistical use. As explained earlier, your personal computer might be able to create a scientific calculator. Most of the functions below will be found on any scientific calculator, but function keys may have to be pressed to access these functions.

Fraction to Decimal Conversion AND Percentages

If you have a calculator, these tables are unnecessary, since by dividing the top of any fraction by the bottom, you automatically convert the fraction to a decimal.

Read the above again, since it is the key to understanding fraction to decimal conversion.

Where fractions can be reduced, look at the reduced equivalent. For example, neither $^4/_{32}$ nor $^2/_{16}$ are in the table below, since each are the same as $^1/_8$. To reduce a fraction, divide the top and bottom of the fraction by the same amount.

Memorization tip: it is worth memorizing most of these conversions. It saves a lot of keying in time with the calculator and provides an instant solution to many problems. Just as with learning multiplication tables up to 20 times 20, some concentrated effort now will pay dividends for the rest of your life. Learn each conversion just as you would learn a multiplication table, by repetition and rote. Say the conversions aloud, breaking the work into small groups, and ensure that you have learned each group properly before moving on. As with all memorization, revise regularly until the knowledge is permanent and comes instantly to mind without effort.

Look for patterns in the digits after the decimal point. Remember that if you forget any of the figures when you don't have the table to hand, you can check the conversion by dividing the top of a fraction by the bottom. Thus, with $^3/_{32}$, for example, $3 \div 32 = 0.09375$:

$$
\begin{array}{r}
0.09375 \\
32\overline{)3.00000} \\
288 \\
\hline
120 \\
96 \\
\hline
240 \\
224 \\
\hline
160 \\
160 \\
\hline
0
\end{array}
$$

Or you can simply key 3 ÷ 32 into your calculator.

Conversion chart

(Where repeating digits are present, rounding to 2 decimalplaces has been done)

$1/1 =$	1	$1/2 =$	0.5	$1/11 =$ 0.0909		$2/11 =$ 0.1818
				$3/11 =$ 0.2727		$4/11 =$ 0.3636
$1/3 =$	0.33	$2/3 =$	0.66	$5/11 =$ 0.4545		$6/11 =$ 0.5454
				$7/11 =$ 0.6361		$8/11 =$ 0.7272
$1/4 =$	0.25	$3/4 =$	0.75	$9/11 =$ 0.8181		$10/11 =$ 0.9090

$1/5 =$ 0.2 $2/5 =$ 0.4 $1/12 =$ 0.083 $5/12 =$ 0.416

$3/5 =$ 0.6 $4/5 =$ 0.8 $7/12 =$ 0.583 $11/12 =$ 0.916

$1/6 =$ 0.16 $5/6 =$ 0.83 $1/16 =$ 0.0625 $3/16 =$ 0.1875

                                           $5/16 =$ 0.3125 $7/16 =$ 0.4375

$1/7 =$ 0.142857 $2/7 =$ 0.285714 $9/16 =$ 0.5625 $11/16 =$ 0.6875

$3/7 =$ 0.428571 $4/7 =$ 0.571428 $13/16 =$ 0.8125 $15/16 =$ 0.9375

$5/7 =$ 0.714285 $6/7 =$ 0.857142

                                           $1/32 =$ 0.03125 $3/32 =$ 0.09375

$1/8 =$ 0.125 $3/8 =$ 0.375 $5/32 =$ 0.15625 $7/32 =$ 0.21875

$5/8 =$ 0.625 $7/8 =$ 0.875 $9/32 =$ 0.28125 $11/32 =$ 0.34375

                                           $13/32 =$ 0.40625 $15/32 =$ 0.46875

$1/9 =$ 0.11 $2/9 =$ 0.22 $17/32 =$ 0.53125 $19/32 =$ 0.59375

$4/9 =$ 0.44 $5/9 =$ 0.55 $21/32 =$ 0.65625 $23/32 =$ 0.71875

$7/9 =$ 0.77 $8/9 =$ 0.88 $25/32 =$ 0.78125 $27/32 =$ 0.84375

                                           $29/32 =$ 0.90625 $31/32 =$ 0.96875

$1/10 =$ 0.1 $3/10 =$ 0.3

$7/10 =$ 0.7 $9/10 =$ 0.9

Converting decimals back into fractions

Any decimal can be immediately expressed as a fraction by putting it on top of a 1 followed by as many 0s as necessary. It is then simply a matter of reducing the fraction by dividing the top and bottom by the same amount. (It is not alway possible to come to a perfect solution because of the inaccurate nature of decimals which have been abbreviated.)

For example, convert 0.375 into a fraction.

1. Put **375** over **1000** = $^{375}/_{1000}$ (1 plus the same number of zeros as the number of places after the decimal point)

2. Divide both top and bottom by **5** = $^{75}/_{200}$
(because it is easier to start this way)

3. Divide both top and bottom again, this time by **25** = $^{3}/_{8}$

Now do some of your own.

Converting fractions into percentages

When you work out percentages you will see that a percentage answer is similar to a decimal number, if you move the decimal point two places to the right. So, just as you have learned the table on page 48, now you can work out percentages. This is because 100% of a number is equal to all of that number, i.e. multiplying it by 1.

For example: What percentage of **11** is **4**.

If you use a calculator you would key **4, ÷ (or /), 11, × (or *), 100,** and **=**. You will get **36.363636363636**. $^{4}/_{11}$ quoted as a decimal is **0.363636363636**.

CALENDAR WIZARD

It is possible to work out the day of the week for any date from January 1, 1725 to December 31, 2099. This trick can be done mentally by anyone with a good head for figures. You can note the table down on a card and refer to it to work out your answer, but if you want to really impress people, memorize the table and practise doing the calculations in your head. If you work out the birthday days of a few friends, you will soon know the table without even trying to memorize it.

Find the day of the week an event took place (1725 or later) or will occur.

January	1 (0)*	1725–1799	4	Sunday	1
February	4 (3)*	1800s	2	Monday	2
March	4	1900s	0	Tuesday	3
April	0	2000s	6	Wednesday	4
May	2			Thursday	5
June	5			Friday	6
July	0			Saturday	0
August	3				
September	6				
October	1				
November	4				
December	6				

*For leap years use the figures in brackets.

Method

a) Write the last two digits of the year.

b) Divide result from (a) by 4 and omit remainder

c) Enter the month code, remembering to take into account if it is a leap year (a Leap Year is divisible by 4 without remainder).

d) Enter the date of the month.

e) Enter the century code.

f) Add results from (a), (b), (c), (d), and (e).

g) Divide result from (f) by 7 and put the remainder in a circle.

h) Enter day for this remainder.

Example:

Find the day of the week when slavery was abolished in America, December 18, 1862.

a) Last 2 digits = 62   62
b) Divide (a) by 4 and delete remainder: 62 ÷ 4 = 15 (remainder 2)   15
c) Month code (not relevant to Leap Year): December = 5   5
d) Enter date of month = 18th   18
e) Enter century code = 1800s   2   ____
f) Add (a) + (b) + (c) + (d) + (e): 15 + 5 + 18 + 2 = 40   102
g) Divide (f) by 7: 102 ÷ 7 = 14, with remainder of 4
h) Check remainder code 4 to get day. **4 = Wednesday**

Therefore, slavery was abolished in America on Wednesday December 18, 1862.

CALENDAR WIZARD PUZZLES

1. Find the day of the week when President John F. Kennedy was assassinated: November 22, 1963.

a) Last 2 digits = —   —
b) Divide (a) by 4 and delete remainder: — ÷ 4 = — (remainder —)   —
c) Month code: —
d) Enter date of month   —
e) Enter century code   —
f) Add (a) + (b) + (c) + (d) + (e): — + — + — + — + — = ——   ____
g) Divide (f) by 7: — ÷ 7 = —, with remainder of —
h) Check remainder code — to get day. — = ...day

✔ *Turn to page 53 for the answers*

2. Find the day of the week when Prince Charles married Lady Diana: July 29, 1981.

a) Last 2 digits = —   —

b) Divide (a) by 4 and delete remainder: — ÷ 4 = — (remainder —)   —

c) Month code: —

d) Enter date of month   —

e) Enter century code   —

f) Add (a) + (b) + (c) + (d) + (e): — + — + — + — + — = —   ——

g) Divide (f) by 7: — ÷ 7 = —, with remainder of —   ——

h) Check remainder code — to get day. — = ...day

3. Find the day of the week when the poet T.S. Eliot was born: September 26, 1888.

a) Last 2 digits = —   —

b) Divide (a) by 4 and delete remainder: — ÷ 4 = — (remainder —)   —

c) Month code: —

d) Enter date of month   —

e) Enter century code   —

f) Add (a) + (b) + (c) + (d) + (e): — + — + — + — + — = —   ——

g) Divide (f) by 7: — ÷ 7 = —, with remainder of —   ——

h) Check remainder code — to get day. — = ...day

4. Find the day of the week when the USA ice hockey team won the gold medal at the Winter Olympic Games: February 24, 1980.

a) Last 2 digits = —   —

b) Divide (a) by 4 and delete remainder: — ÷ 4 = — (remainder —)   —

c) Month code: —

d) Enter date of month   —

e) Enter century code   —

f) Add (a) + (b) + (c) + (d) + (e): — + — + — + — + — = —   ——

g) Divide (f) by 7: — ÷ 7 = —, with remainder of —   ——

h) Check remainder code — to get day. — = ...day

CALENDAR WIZARD ANSWERS

1.

Friday.

(a) 63	63
(b) 63 ÷ 4 = 15 (remainder 3)	15
(c) November = 4 (Leap Year does not apply)	4
(d) Date = 22	22
(e) Century code = 0	0
(f) Sum of (a) + (b) + (c) + (d) + (e): 63 + 15 + 4 + 22 + 0	104
(g) Sum of (f) ÷ 7. 104 ÷ 7 = 14 (remainder 6)	
(h) 6 = Friday	

2.

Wednesday.

(a) 81	81
(b) 81 ÷ 4 = 20 (remainder 1)	20
(c) July = 0 (Leap Year does not apply)	0
(d) Date = 29	29
(e) Century code = 0	0
(f) Sum of (a) + (b) + (c) + (d) + (e): 81 + 20 + 0 + 29 + 0	130
(g) Sum of (f) ÷ 7. 130 ÷ 7 = 18 (remainder 4)	
(h) 4 = Wednesday	

3.

Wednesday.

(a) 88	88
(b) 88 ÷ 4 = 22 (remainder 0)	22
(c) September = 6 (Leap Year does not apply)	6
(d) Date = 26	26
(e) Century code = 2	2
(f) Sum of (a) + (b) + (c) + (d) + (e): 88 + 22 + 6 + 26 + 2	144
(g) Sum of (f) ÷ 7. 144 ÷ 7 = 20 remainder 4)	
(h) 4 = Wednesday	

4.

Sunday.

(a) 80	80
(b) 80 ÷ 4 = 20 (remainder 0)	20
(c) February = 3 (Leap Year applies)	3
(d) Date = 24	24
(e) Century code = 0	0
(f) Sum of (a) + (b) + (c) + (d) + (e): 0 + 20 + 3 + 24 + 21	27
(g) Sum of (f) ÷ 7. 127 ÷ 7 = 18 (remainder 1)	
(h) 1 = Sunday	

SOME FASCINATING FACTS ABOUT CIRCLES

How many circles are here?

Solution 18 circles.

π pronounced and sometimes written "pi" (pronounced like cottage pie) is a strange and magical number that is equal to the circumference divided by the diameter of any circle. We can use π to work out the area of a circle, using the formula, πr^2 This means π times the radius squared, so when we find the radius of a circle, we multiply it by itself, then by π, and we know the area of that circle. At the end of this section there are some problems based around this principle.

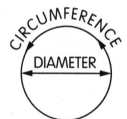

$$\pi = \frac{circumference}{diameter}$$

Nobody has ever worked out the full number for π, so it is not known if π continues for ever or develops a pattern of repetition at a certain point. π expressed as a fraction is approximately $^{22}/_{7}$. Here is π calculated to the first 100 digits. If you can do this, even with the help of a computer, you must be a real maths wizard. For most purposes it is sufficient to use 3.142 as an approximation, but it has been calculated to around a billion digits so far.

π = 3.1415926535 8979323846 2643383279 5028841971 6939937510 5820974944 5923078164 0628620899 8628034825 3421170679 ... and so on.

Tip:

Circles are always round. If you squash a circle down, it stops being a circle, and becomes an oval.

Here are some definitions of circle elements:

Arc

A curved line that is part of the circumference of a circle.

Chord

A line inside a circle that touches 2 points on the circle.

Circumference

The distance around the circle. Found by the formula π x diameter.

Diameter

The distance across a circle at its widest point.

Origin

The exact middle of the circle.

Radius

The distance from the origin of the circle to any point on it.

Sector

Like a slice of pizza (a wedge). The inside angle of a sector is used to determine the area of the sector. Since every circle has 360°, the proportion of the angle to 360° will be the same as the proportion of the area of the sector to the total area of the circle.

Tangent of circle

A line perpendicular to the radius that touches only one point of the circle.

Here is a handy guide for calculating the radius, circumference, and diameters of circles.

$$c = \pi \times d$$
$$d = \frac{c}{\pi}$$
$$\pi = \frac{c}{d}$$

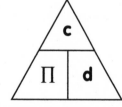

STRANGE FACT

Did you know that circles exist in only two dimensions?
Circles are concepts, and, unlike the real world, have no thickness. The ink that the circle is drawn from is not the circle. Only the idea in your mind is the circle.

CIRCLE PUZZLES

All the information you need to solve these problems is given in this chapter.

Your answers should be rounded to two decimal places where necessary.

1. Find the area of a circle with a radius of 10.

2. If 25% of a circle has an area of 13, what is the area of the circle?

3. Find the radius of a circle with an area of 40.

4. If 10% of a circle has an area of 30, what is the diameter?

5. What is the radius of a circle with a diameter of 8?

6. If half the area of a circle is 15, what is the radius?

7. Find the area of a circle with a radius of π.

8. A 60° sector of a circle has an area of 20. What is the area of the entire circle?

9. The circumference of a circle is 10. What is the diameter?

10. The radius of a circle is 18. What is the circumference?

11. How many more small circles will fit inside this triangle?

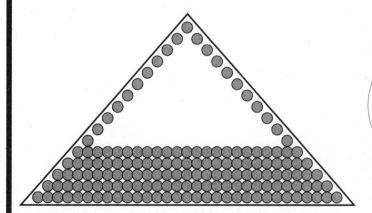

12. How many circles are here?

✔ *Turn to page 58 for the answers*

CIRCLE ANSWERS

1.
314.16. $\pi \times 10^2$.

2.
52. 13 x 4, since 25% is a quarter.

3.
3.57. $\pi r^2 = 40$; $r^2 = 40 \div \pi$;
$r = \sqrt{(40 \div \pi)} = 3.57$.

4.
19.54. $\pi r^2 = 300$. From 10 x 30;
$r^2 = 300 \div \pi$; $r = \sqrt{(300 \div \pi)}$ [9.77].
The diameter is (2 x r) [9.77] x 2 = 19.54.

5.
4. 8 ÷ 2.

6.
3.09. $\pi r^2 = 30$; 2 x 15;
$r^2 = 30 \div \pi$; $r = \sqrt{(30 \div \pi)} = 3.09$.

7.
31. Because radius (r) = π,
then $\pi r^2 = \pi \times \pi^2 = 31$.

8.
120. A 60° sector is one-sixth of a full circle, so 6 x 20 =120.

9.
3.18. Diameter = circumference ÷ π = 10 ÷ π = 3.18.

10.
113.10.
Circumference = π x diameter = π x 2 x 18 = π x 36 = 113.10.

11.
100. Each row has 2 less than the row below it.

12.
There are 20 circles.

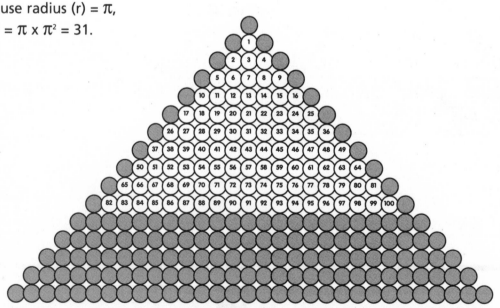

FIVE TOUGH TESTS

Puzzle 1

Two cars 200 miles apart are moving toward each other; each one is going at a speed of 50 miles per hour. A hornet starting on the front of one of them flies back and forth between them at a rate of 75 miles per hour. It does this until the cars collide and crush the hornet to death. What is the total distance the hornet has flown?

Puzzle 2

If you take a 5-digit number, reverse it, and subtract the result from the original number, you are left with 21978. If only the digits 2, 4, 6, 8 are used, what was the original number?

Puzzle 3

Jilly has a number of cards. If she deals them equally between 4 people, she has 2 left. If she deals them equally between 7 people, she has 4 left. If she deals them equally between 3 people, she has 10 left. How many cards are in the pack?

Puzzle 4

Find these two 4 digit numbers:

The square of the first, plus the second, equals 97540808.
The square of the second, plus the first, equals 29516500.

Puzzle 5

Find this eight-digit number:

The first 4 digits – the last 4 digits = 2222. The middle 4 digits added together total 10. Only the digits 1,2,3 & 4 are used.

✔ *Turn to page 66 for the answer*

SECRET CODES

Alphanumeric Code

This is a simple code, but still takes time to solve, and it is suitable for secret communications between friends when it is unlikely that anyone else in the house would be able to solve the code if they came across one of the secret notes.

Choose any letter of the alphabet, and the code is based on that. When you have set up this code with a friend, ensure that the friend knows that the last (or first) letter of the note is the one that is being used to code this letter.

For example, a "d" code would add 3 to the alphanumberical value of each letter in the note; a becomes d; b becomes e, roll over at "z".

1	2	3	4	5	6	7	8	9	10	11	12	13	14	15	16	17	18	19	20	21	22	23	24	25	26
a	b	c	d	e	f	g	h	i	j	k	l	m	n	o	p	q	r	s	t	u	v	w	x	y	z
d	e	f	g	h	i	j	k	l	m	n	o	p	q	r	s	t	u	v	w	x	y	z	a	b	c

Thus, the message:

> "Dear Billie, meet me on Saturday at the Mall at ten am. See you — Anned"

would become:

> "ghdu eloolh, phhw ph rq vdwxugdb dw wkh pdoo dw whq dp. vhh brx — dqqhd."

Note that the key letter "d", which has been added to the end of Anne's name, is left unchanged. Sometimes you don't have to add a keyletter because the last or first letter of your note works in well as the keyletter.

Alternatively, you can agree a position for the key letter with the person sending or receiving the note. For example, you could agree that the letter in 15th position on your note would always be the key letter. This would force anyone trying to break your code to try out a lot of options before hitting on the correct solution.

Also note that no capitals are used in the coded words — they can be too much of a givaway.

Some people go a stage further and group all the letters into packets of 4, and remove all punctuation.

E.g. "ghdu eloo lhph hwph rqvd wxug dbdw wkhp dood wwhq dpvh hbrx dqqhd."

This makes it more difficult to realize that a simple alphanumeric code has been used, because it is a fairly easy matter to go through all the two letter words commonly used and try out various solutions on them to see if they resolve to *it*, *to*, *of*, *is*, or *on*. When you find the solution to one word, using this code, you have the solution to the whole thing.

Multiplicand Code

A more difficult to break code can be made by multiplying the alphanumerical value of the letters in your note by a six digit number. In order to be certain of solving the code, assuming you somehow knew that this was the type of code involved, you'd have to try 899,999 options as divisors. But as with all these types of codes, if you have a clue what any of the words are you can find a solution by dividing the numbers by a figure that arrives at the alphanumeric position.

For example, one of the most commonly used words of the English language becomes:
15789120 6315648 3947280

The solution is found by dividing each set of numbers by the key number **789456** to get **20 8 5** – **"the"**.

Breaking the Multiplicand Code

If you have to crack a multiplicand coded message, and you don't know the key number, you have no alternative but trial and error. First of all you have to figure out how many digits are in the multiplicand. If you don't know how many digits are being used, but you do know it is a multiplicand code, you need to try the following with all possible numbers of digits until a solution is found.

Guessing at words.

It's a fair guess that the word *the* will be a component of most messages. If we know that each group of numbers stands for a letter, we can pick, by trial and error, on three consecutive groups and test them to see if we can reveal *the*. Since the letter t is 20th in the alphabet, and e is 5th, looking again at the coded *the* from above,   15789120 6315648 3947280, the difference between the first group 15789120, and the last group 3947280, when divided by 20, will be the same as the difference between 6315648 and 3947280 when divided by 5. We find that this is indeed the case, (473673.6).

Now that we have found *the* we can divide the code number for the letter t — 15789120 by 20 to find the number that we can use to solve any other words in the sentence assuming that the same number has been used on all the words. (Some codes use key numbers that increase proportionally with every word.) Thus we get 789456. We then check the solution by dividing the codes 6315648 3947280 by 789456, to see if we get 8 & 5 respectively. We do.

Many further complications are possible. For example, alphanumerical displacement could be used so that t is represented by 15 rather than 20; h is represented by 3 rather than 8, and e is represented by 2 (roll over) rather than 5. Thus you'd have to recognize the relative displacement positions in order to recognize the word and key solution.

SECRET CODES PUZZLES

1. Decode the following, based on the above method, but using a different keyletter. Also, you have to figure out whether the keyletter is at the end or at the beginning:

dcsfm qcasg bsofsf hc jwhoz hfihv hvob wvghcfm — dzohco

Use the template below to try out your decoding.

1	2	3	4	5	6	7	8	9	10	11	12	13	14	15	16	17	18	19	20	21	22	23	24	25	26
a	b	c	d	e	f	g	h	i	j	k	l	m	n	o	p	q	r	s	t	u	v	w	x	y	z

Solution is Miscellaneous Answer 6.

2. Decode the following, based on the above method, but using a different keycode. Also, you have to figure out if the keycode is embedded in the grouping and whether there is alphanumeric displacement. This is a genius level problem.

Clue:

The key is a six-digit number. Decoded, you will find a quote from a man who was very concerned about the use of time, with one word per line.

1794582	8374716						
7776522	8374716	11365686					
10767492	9571104	11963880	15553044	7776522	1794582	2392776	10169298
11365686	4785552	7178328	2392776				
2990970	8374716	10169298					
11365686	4187358	15553044	11365686				
4785552	10767492						
11365686	4187358	2392776					
10767492	11365686	11963880	2990970	2990970			
6580134	4785552	2990970	2392776				
4785552	10767492						
7178328	15553044	1794582	2392776				
8374716	2990970						
598194	2392776	8374716	5383746	15553044	7178328	4785552	8374716
2990970	10169298	15553044	7776522	5981940	6580134	4785552	7776522

Solution is Miscellaneous Answer 7.

 Turn to page 66 for the answers

Use the following templates to try out your decoding.

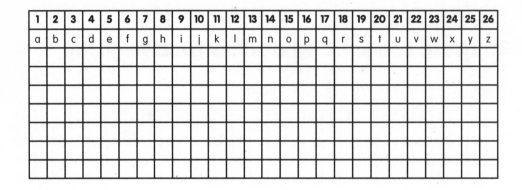

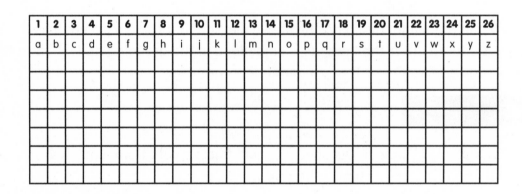

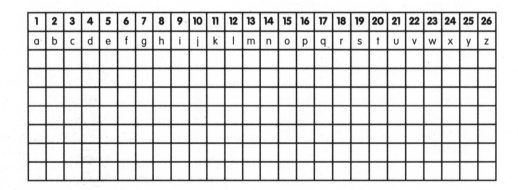

1	2	3	4	5	6	7	8	9	10	11	12	13	14	15	16	17	18	19	20	21	22	23	24	25	26
a	b	c	d	e	f	g	h	i	j	k	l	m	n	o	p	q	r	s	t	u	v	w	x	y	z

1	2	3	4	5	6	7	8	9	10	11	12	13	14	15	16	17	18	19	20	21	22	23	24	25	26
a	b	c	d	e	f	g	h	i	j	k	l	m	n	o	p	q	r	s	t	u	v	w	x	y	z

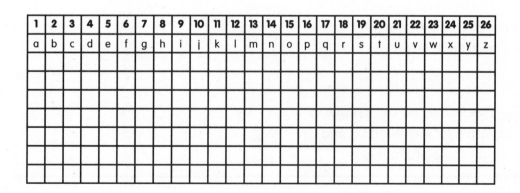

1	2	3	4	5	6	7	8	9	10	11	12	13	14	15	16	17	18	19	20	21	22	23	24	25	26
a	b	c	d	e	f	g	h	i	j	k	l	m	n	o	p	q	r	s	t	u	v	w	x	y	z

MISCELLANEOUS ANSWERS

1.

150 miles. The cars are 200 miles apart and each car is doing 50 miles an hour, so it takes 2 hours for the cars to collide. Therefore, the hornet must have flown for two hours too and as it was flying at a rate of 75 miles per hour, the hornet must have flown 150 miles.

2

84626. 84626 - 62648 = 21978

3

46 (46 / 4 = 11r2; 46 / 7=6r4;
46 / 3=12r10)

4.

9876 & 5432 (9876^2 = 97535376; 97535376 + 5432 = 97540808; 5432^2 = 29506624; 29506624 + 9876 = 29516500)

5.

44332211

1	2	3	4	5	6	7	8	9	10	11	12	13	14	15	16	17	18	19	20	21	22	23	24	25	26
a	b	c	d	e	f	g	h	i	j	k	l	m	n	o	p	q	r	s	t	u	v	w	x	y	z
o	p	q	r	s	t	u	v	w	x	y	z	a	b	c	d	e	f	g	h	i	j	k	l	m	n

6.

Poetry comes nearer to vital truth than history. — Plato (Code letter o).

7.

Key number 598194. Divide each supplied code number with the key number, and then add1 to get the alphanumeric equivalent of:
"Do not squander time, for that is the stuff life is made of." — Benjamin Franklin.

Note that the keynumber was embedded in the code.

BEAT THE CALCULATOR!

(No, not with a stick!)

Here's how you can amaze your friends by beating a calculator to the answer of a three-part addition sum every time.

Step 1. Ask a friend to write down a five-digit number
(it works with longer or shorter numbers too).

e.g. 31625

Step 2. Immediately below your friend's number, working from left to right (so that it will not be obvious that you are subtracting) put down the numbers which, when added to each above digit will make 9.

31625
68374

(You are saying to yourself, "**3** from **9** is **6**; **1** from **9** is **8**; **6** from **9** is **3**; **2** from **9** is **7**; and **5** from **9** is **4**." When added together the two numbers equal **99999**.)

Step 3. Now ask your friend to write down another five-digit number below your number.

31625
68374
73840

Step 4. Hand your friend a calculator and say,
"Okay, start calculating the total of the three numbers."

Step 5. As your friend is still keying in the digits, you will immediately be able to write the correct answer.

173839

The answer to the sum is always the last number that your friend wrote down, with a 1 in front (making, in this case, a six-digit number), and 1 subtracted from the last digit (or two digits if the last one is a zero). In the example shown, the last number was a 0, so we subtracted 1 from 40 to give 39.

Now try a few yourself. To make the trick convincing you have to get really good at subtracting from 9, so that it will not be obvious that you are calculating.

MEMORIZING STUFF

The more you use your ability to memorize, the better you will get at it. Think of your memory as a muscle that gets stronger the more you use it. There is enough space in your brain to memorize everything that has ever been known, and still have room for more.

Start practising your memorization by learning this commonly used little rhyme to recall the number of days in every month. You'll find it very useful not to have to refer to a calender for this information.

Thirty days has September,

April, June and November.

All the rest have thirty-one

Except February alone,

Which has but twenty-eight days clear

And twenty-nine in each leap-year.

Important dates can be memorized in a similar way with the help of rhymes. For example, most people know that

"In 1492 Columbus sailed the ocean blue."

Studies have shown that the best way to memorize for long-term recall is :

• Take information in small chunks, using a sheet of paper to cover over the stuff you haven't yet got to, and repeat it over and over until you have it right.

• Repeat the information aloud, or at least under your breath.

• Before moving on to the next piece, go back over everything you are currently memorizing from the beginning. Thus, when you are memorizing a table, start back from the beginning when you've learned a new chunk.

• Don't go onto new material until you have perfectly repeated what you are learning at least three times, (from the beginning).

• Take frequent breaks. Stop for at least five minutes every half-hour.

• Once you have memorized something perfectly, revise the material regularly to make it permanent in your brain. (See the revision chart later in this section.)

• Don't stop your revisions once you are sure that you know the material, but gradually extend the time interval between revisions until you only need check it once every few months. You'll soon know if you've started to forget, and you'll be able to work some extra revisions into your plan.

Here's another to memorize:

In October 14th, 1066,
Harold the Second was taught some new tricks
by William the First, who beat him hands down
at the Battle of Hastings, where they fought for the crown.

For those involved in trigonometry, the rules of SINE, COSINE, and TANGENT can be difficult to recall without an mnemonic (pronounced knee-mon-ick – a memory device).

SIN = Opposite/Hypotenuse
COS = Adjacent/Hypotenuse
TAN = Opposite/Adjacent

Some people can remember this using the acronym (the first letters) alone, as a word, SOHCAHTOA, pronounced So-ka-toe-ah.

Or you could use:

Some **O**ld **H**eavy
Cows **A**re **H**eavier
Than **O**thers **A**re

When you recall the first letter, it brings to mind the word you are trying to recall with the same first letter. You repeat the verse to yourself and write down the letters as you recall them. For example: Some Old Heavy =>> Sine = Opposite over Hypotenuse.

Memorize the following, if you don't already know the facts which they illuminate:

There are three hundred and sixty purple degrees in a circle

Rhymes don't have to work very well to be remembered!

Every **R**ight **A**ngle **E**quals **N**inety **D**egrees.
Eskimos **R**eally **A**re **E**ating **N**ice **D**inners.

You can combine acronyms with other words to make memorable sentences. When making up mnemonic devices it is best to make them as ridiculous as possible. Ridiculous phrases stick in the mind better than everyday phrases.

Inside **A**ngles of a **T**riangle **A**lways **A**dd to **O**ne **H**undred and **E**ighty.
IATAA (**I a**te **A**n) **OHE** (**O**ld **H**airy **E**gg)
I Ate **A**n **O**ld **H**airy **E**gg.

Many people get mixed up with millimetres, centimetres and metres.

Here's a little mnemonic poem to help you recall the relationships.

Every kilometre has a thousand metres
It's not like measuring in inches and feetres.

There's a hundred cents in every dollar
A hundred centimetres makes
a metre collar.

And in every centimetre there are ten
Tiny millimetre measuring men.

Use the following space to list some things you'd like to be able to recall and make up your own verses or acronyms to memorize them:

_____
_____
_____
_____
_____
_____
_____
_____
_____
_____
_____
_____
_____
_____
_____
_____

MEMORIZING NUMBERS

You get better at this with practice. After a glance at a list of numbers, most people can recall at least some of them. Test your own ability with the following list of random numbers. Cover the list with a sheet of paper and slide it down the list one at a time, reading each row just once, then close your eyes, count aloud to 10, then repeat the number. If you got it wrong, try again. If you got it right, pass down to the next number and continue the process. See how many digits you can reproduce correctly.

1. 7
2. 69
3. 990
4. 3034
5. 24389
6. 111952
7. 0873803
8. 24007903
9. 231886744
10. 9605603462
11. 78360120741
12. 298567021023
13. 0756023567130
14. 04738567286024
15. 905467193419235
16. 1119347953283294
17. 30076490981224573
18. 342165677385427832
19. 0453265677808729780
20. 832098765232347893 59

How did you do?

1 –3

Not too good; keep on working at it

4 –8

Not bad

8 –12

Very high

13 –16

Extraordinary

17 –20

Unbelievable!

Grouping

One effective way to memorize long numbers is to group them into chunks.So instead of having to say to yourself for 193745, "One, nine, three, seven, four, five," you can break the number into 19, 37, 45 — "Nineteen, thirty-seven, forty-five."

This has the effect of making you need to remember only three numbers instead of six. For some people it might be too much to go a step further and just use two chunks: "A hundred and ninety-three, seven hundred and forty-five."

Go back to the list above now and see how much further you get by grouping the digits into chunks. Many people will go up a grade.

By gauging your performance you will be able to see whether it is better for you to group larger numbers into chunks of 2 or 3 digits.

5-DAY CARD FILE MEMORIZATION

This is an excellent way to memorize passages of text and formulae for exams. By gradually increasing the time period between readings you force your memory to stretch itself every time. Never refer to a card until you have tried your best to recall what is on the card.

A word of warning though. If you feel that you are making a mistake, refer to the card immediately. If you don't do this, and you spend a lot of time memorizing the mistake, you may always have trouble trying to tell the right version from the wrong version.

Day 1

Step 1

Make a 3 x 5 card for each passage or item you want to commit to memory. Any size card will do if you can't get these. Blank business cards or indexing cards are great for the job.

Step 2

In the upper left hand corner write the subject, such as "Simple equations."

Step 3

In the body of the card write the text. At the bottom you may wish to add cross references, but don't make it too complicated.

Step 4

Begin with just one subject and one card. Read aloud. Keep up a steady rhythm. Read the first card five times. We'll call that a "set". At the end of each reading, or each set, mark the back of the card to indicate a complete set. Repeat this five times throughout the day. By the end of the day you will have read the card twenty-five times.
After every reading, go as far as you can in recalling the details without looking until you make a mistake.

Day 2

Add a second card with a new passage or item to memorize. After five days you will be working with five cards in the memorization process, and the balance of cards in a "maintenance" process.

Repeat day one's activity with the new card.
Perform five sets on card two.
Perform four sets on card one.

Day 3

Repeat day two's activity with a new card.
Perform five sets on card three.
Perform four sets on card two.
Perform three sets on card one.

Day 4

Repeat day three's activity with a new card.
Perform five sets on card four.
Perform four sets on card three.
Perform three sets on card two.
Perform two sets on card one.

Day 5

Repeat day four's activity with a new card.
Perform five sets on card five.
Perform four sets on card four.
Perform three sets on card three.
Perform two sets on card two.
Perform one set on card one.

Thus the pattern emerges. Continue adding cards each day in the same way. When a card is five days old it gets read for just one set. On the sixth day, you read it only once.

Move the card into maintenance mode

After you read a card on the sixth day, put it in a stack that you pick up and review once a month or so. If you find that you are forgetting details you can put a card back through the 5 day cycle.

On day 6, since you are finished with one card for the time being, you can add a new card at the beginning of the cycle. Thus there is a continuous rotation of cards and you can continue the program of memorization.

Other Memorization Tricks

Use Visualization and Linking

For example, if you want to recall the formula for a circle, πr^2 think of a huge square pie with circles coming out of the hole in the middle that steam would normally come from.

If you need to remember the number 40, you could link it with an image of a golfer shouting, "Forty," rather than, "Fore."

If you need to recall the formula for speed: Speed = distance/time, (s=d/t) put the elements into a triangle. In this way you can easily see the relationship between the different variables.

Speed and time are beside each other, so distance = speed * time.
Looking at the triangle, distance can be visualized over time, so speed = distance/time.

Looking at the triangle, below, from the point of view of time, distance can be visualized over speed, so time = distance / speed.

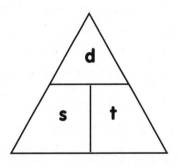

MEMORIZING MULTIPLICATION TABLES

(Up to 20 x 20)

Why bother learning multiplication tables up to 20 times 20? There are three reasons:

1. Instantly knowing the answer to the multiplications in these tables will save you time, not only during tests in every branch of maths, physics and chemistry, but for the rest of your life.

2. It's a great mental exercise to get your brain into peak mathematical shape.

3. You'll impress your teachers, parents and friends. More importantly, you'll prove to yourself that you can do it. If you have the persistence to learn these tables you'll be capable of anything.

If they want to, 10-year-olds can learn these tables in five days (plus the reinforcement period) using the card file memorization system outlined overleaf. With kids younger than 10, it may take two sessions of the system to permanently memorize the tables.

Read across the tables when learning, reading one item every second, with a pause of one second between items.

E.g.: "Four twos – eight. Four threes – twelve. Four fours – sixteen."

1	2	3	4	5	6	7	8	9	10	11	12	13	14	15	16	17	18	19	20
2	**4**	6	8	10	12	14	16	18	20	22	24	26	28	30	32	34	36	38	40
3	6	**9**	12	15	18	21	24	27	30	33	36	39	42	45	48	51	54	57	60
4	8	12	**16**	20	24	28	32	36	40	44	48	52	56	60	64	68	72	76	80
5	10	15	20	**25**	30	35	40	45	50	55	60	65	70	75	80	85	90	95	100
6	12	18	24	30	**36**	42	48	54	60	66	72	78	84	90	96	102	108	114	120
7	14	21	28	35	42	**49**	56	63	70	77	84	91	98	105	112	119	126	133	140
8	16	24	32	40	48	56	**64**	72	80	88	96	104	112	120	128	136	144	152	160
9	18	27	36	45	54	63	72	**81**	90	99	108	117	126	135	144	153	162	171	180
10	20	30	40	50	60	70	80	90	**100**	110	120	130	140	150	160	170	180	190	200
11	22	33	44	55	66	77	88	99	110	**121**	132	143	154	165	176	187	198	209	220
12	24	36	48	60	72	84	96	108	120	132	**144**	156	168	180	192	204	216	228	240
13	26	39	52	65	78	91	104	117	130	143	156	**169**	182	195	208	221	234	247	260
14	28	42	56	70	84	98	112	126	140	154	168	182	**196**	210	224	238	252	266	280
15	30	45	60	75	90	105	120	135	150	165	180	195	210	**225**	240	255	270	285	300
16	32	48	64	80	96	112	128	144	160	176	192	208	224	240	**256**	272	288	304	320
17	34	51	68	85	102	119	136	153	170	187	204	221	238	255	272	**289**	306	323	340
18	36	54	72	90	108	126	144	162	180	198	216	234	252	270	288	306	**324**	342	360
19	38	57	76	95	114	133	152	171	190	209	228	247	266	285	304	323	342	**361**	380
20	40	60	80	100	120	140	160	180	200	220	240	260	280	300	320	340	360	380	**400**

As an added tip, the perfect squares (2 x 2, 3 x 3, etc.) have been put in a bolder type.

EUCLID

Euclid was the most important teacher of maths who has ever lived. His famous book, The Elements has been in print (hand-written before the development of print) for around 2000 years and has influenced millions of people. He taught at and founded a school at Alexandria in Egypt when Ptolemy I Soter reigned that ancient land, from 323 to c.283 BC.

The Elements contains axioms and definitions, of which the following are some of the best known:

Euclid's axioms

a) Given two points, there is an interval that joins them.

b) An interval can be prolonged indefinitely.

c) A circle can be constructed when its centre and a point on it are given.

d) All right angles are equal.

e) If a straight line falling on two straight lines makes the interior angles on the same side less than two right angles, the two straight lines, if extended indefinitely, meet on that side on which the angles are less than two right angles.

Euclid's Common Notions

(i) Things equal to the same thing are equal.

(ii) If equals are added to equals, the results are equal.

(iii) If equals are subtracted from equals, the remainders are equal.

(iv) Things that coincide with one another are equal.

Let's prove them:

1. Given two points, there is an interval that joins them.

See if you can measure the distance between these points.

●   ●

After trying that, most people will agree that there is an "interval" – a space between the points. Otherwise, it could not be measured.

2. An interval can be prolonged indefinitely.

Test this by making a spot in this circle.

Now make another spot on a sheet of paper across the room. (Not on the wallpaper!) Now imagine putting that sheet of paper into a space rocket and firing it into space far beyond the Milky Way. By doing this, you will be prolonging the interval indefinitely.

3. A circle can be constructed when its centre and a point on it are given.

To test this, use a pair of compasses, and set the compasses as shown. Now make a circle.

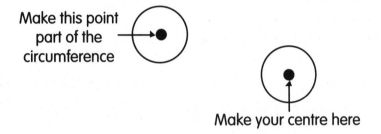

Make this point part of the circumference

Make your centre here

You should end up with something that looks like this:

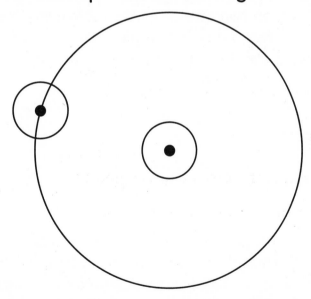

If you've done that, you've shown that Euclid was correct to say that a circle could be made when its centre and a point on it were given.

4. All right angles are equal.

Test this by comparing the right angles on the following objects. You can trace them and compare them with each other, or you can check them with a protractor.

If you found that all the 90° angles in the above were equal, you have shown that Euclid was correct.

5. If a straight line falling on two straight lines makes the interior angles on the same side less than two right angles, the two straight lines, if extended indefinitely, meet on that side on which the angles are less than two right angles.

Looking at the above diagram we can see that, on the marked side where the balls are, the two interior angles are less than right angles (less than 90°) and that when we extend the lines they do actually meet. Thus, Euclid has been proved correct again.

Now take some time to prove Euclid's Common Notions.

CAPTURE ODDS AND EVENS GAME

Players: 2

Requirements:
Capture board.
Pencils and paper.
Player 1 uses a red or black pencil.
player 2 uses a blue or green pencil.
Calculators not needed.

How the game works

1. Player 1 draws a line through any two numbers to start, and then through as many even numbers as possible, without going through any odd numbers. For the purposes of the game, zero is to be used as an even number.

2. Player 2 draws a line through any two numbers to start, and then through as many odd numbers as possible, without going through any even numbers.

3. On the next move players continue from either end of their last move, making as many moves as necessary to get through the blocking squares before having to stick to either odd or even numbers again. Lines may not be crossed.

4. The object is to encircle (capture) by looping right round the other player, and getting back to your starting square or by enclosing the other player against a side of the puzzle. If no captures are made, the player with the highest total value line wins.

5. Players can gain a big advantage by using the other player's numbers (odd or even) to start each move if possible, thus leaving the other player less to work with.

In the game example below, player 1 has started on the shaded squares and been blocked by the number 7. Player 2 has started on the black squares and been blocked by a zero. Player 1's best move will be to go down through the 9 to get to the 0, and then down to the 4, left into the next 4, and so on.

```
                2 5 7 7
              6 3 7 0 5 2 0 2
            4 6 0 2 5 6 2 6 7 0
          0 3 5 9 9 6 7 5 0 6 5 5
          4 0 1 3 8 0 8 8 1 9 2 1
        3 9 0 1 7 4 9 6 2 9 0 6 6 9 0 1
        3 1 5 5 9 6 1 5 6 2 7 9 0 0 0 1 5 3
      1 4 6 7 1 2 1 6 5 5 3 1 8 1 9 0 6 2 0 5
      0 8 2 7 3 9 7 8 0 2 2 2 4 1 2 1 5 2 4 1
    7 5 5 5 7 9 0 6 0 5 3 7 7 2 0 2 2 1 7 1 6 7
    5 2 2 7 3 2 1 6 8 8 1 0 3 4 4 6 0 1 6 1 0 5
    3 1 5 0 7 3 6 4 4 0 3 5 8 7 4 6 2 6 0 9 7 3
      0 8 7 2 1 2 7 0 8 6 2 3 4 9 5 7 0 3 7 6
      2 3 6 1 5 3 0 7 3 1 6 4 0 0 6 5 0 3 7 6
        6 6 4 0 6 0 1 0 7 6 8 4 4 2 6 0 0 1
        0 4 7 0 8 1 3 2 1 5 3 6 6 5 7 4
          8 7 4 5 2 5 7 7 0 2 4 3
          8 2 4 1 2 0 5 2 2 9 0 8
            0 5 0 2 7 4 6 6 0 0
            7 9 9 6 9 0 0 9
              8 9 1 5
```

Rules

1. Any player who closes her/his own loop without capturing automatically loses the game.

2. Only vertical and horizontal moves can be made.

3. When a player cannot move during a game, by, for example, getting blocked, that player may begin a new line, but all moves from the old line are lost.

4. Lines cannot be crossed.

Minor Capture Board

```
            5 2 5 7 7 3 5
          6 3 7 0 5 2 0 2 5
        5 4 6 0 2 5 6 2 6 7 0 4 5
        5 0 3 5 9 9 6 7 5 0 6 5 5 0 3
      4 1 4 0 1 3 8 0 8 8 1 9 2 1 4 0 4
    0 3 9 0 1 7 4 9 6 2 9 0 6 6 9 0 1 5 0
    9 4 6 0 8 2 6 5 9 9 4 0 2 1 1 0 8 2 4 0 5
  1 7 1 4 8 8 5 6 2 5 4 6 1 1 2 4 6 1 8 2 5 6 2
5 1 5 0 4 6 1 5 6 4 6 7 4 6 5 7 9 5 6 2 0 5 6 3 0
6 7 3 9 6 9 7 4 7 5 5 4 5 2 6 5 5 9 6 7 5 2 4 1 5
8 8 5 6 2 5 0 8 5 1 0 9 1 5 8 2 5 6 2 1 7 1 4 2 1
9 7 3 0 9 7 2 3 0 6 1 6 1 1 7 5 1 1 7 4 7 1 6 1 0
0 2 6 4 5 4 9 1 6 5 4 9 1 4 5 4 8 4 6 6 9 2 6 0 9
4 7 2 3 6 1 5 3 0 7 3 1 6 4 0 0 6 5 0 3 7 6 5 4 7
6 7 4 6 6 4 0 6 0 1 0 7 6 8 4 4 2 6 0 0 1 6 2 0 0
0 7 1 5 0 4 7 0 8 1 3 2 1 5 3 6 6 5 7 4 6 5 2 8 3
0 8 7 2 5 2 8 7 4 5 2 5 7 7 0 2 4 3 1 6 1 3 6 3 4
  6 7 5 1 6 8 2 4 1 2 0 5 2 2 9 0 8 2 9 1 6 3 4
    0 9 5 1 4 0 5 0 2 7 4 6 6 0 0 1 4 0 7 1 6
      1 6 9 0 1 7 9 9 6 9 0 0 9 5 9 0 1 4 5
        4 0 8 2 8 3 8 9 1 5 1 6 2 0 8 2 5
          7 1 6 2 1 1 6 7 4 1 0 4 7 1 6
            5 4 3 0 9 6 8 2 2 3 6 4 5
              6 7 3 2 4 6 0 7 6
                6 2 5 3 0 6 7
```

Major Capture Board

```
            5 1 5 7 7 0 5
          6 7 3 5 5 2 6 2 5
      5 4 6 0 2 0 6 2 0 7 0 4 5
    5 0 3 5 9 0 5 7 5 1 6 5 5 0 3
  4 1 4 0 1 3 8 6 8 8 0 9 2 1 4 0 4
0 3 9 0 1 7 4 9 0 2 9 2 6 6 9 0 1 5 0
9 4 6 0 8 2 6 5 9 6 4 0 1 1 1 0 8 2 4 0 5
1 7 1 4 8 8 5 6 2 5 9 6 1 5 2 4 6 1 8 2 5 6 2
5 1 5 0 4 6 1 5 6 4 6 4 4 6 6 7 9 5 6 2 0 5 6 3 0
6 7 3 9 6 9 7 4 7 5 5 7 5 2 8 5 5 9 6 7 5 2 4 1 5
8 8 5 6 2 5 0 8 5 1 0 4 1 5 7 2 5 6 2 1 7 1 4 2 1
9 7 3 0 9 7 2 3 0 6 1 9 1 1 5 5 1 1 7 4 7 1 6 1 0
0 2 6 4 5 4 9 1 6 5 4 6 1 4 8 4 8 4 6 6 9 2 6 0 9
8 8 5 6 2 5 0 8 5 1 0 9 5 1 2 5 6 2 1 7 1 4 2 1
0 1 9 7 2 0 9 7 2 3 0 9 1 6 1 1 7 5 1 1 7 4 7 1 6
9 0 0 2 6 4 5 4 9 1 6 6 4 9 0 4 5 4 8 4 6 6 9 2 6
4 7 2 3 6 1 5 3 0 7 3 5 6 4 0 0 6 5 0 3 7 6 5 4 7
4 7 2 3 6 1 5 3 0 7 3 5 6 4 0 0 6 5 0 3 7 6 5 4 7
6 7 4 6 6 4 0 6 0 1 0 1 6 8 3 4 2 6 0 0 1 6 2 0 0
0 7 1 5 0 4 7 0 8 1 3 7 1 5 0 6 6 5 7 4 6 5 2 8 3
0 8 7 2 5 2 8 7 4 5 2 2 7 7 2 2 4 3 1 6 1 3 6 2 1
  6 7 5 1 6 8 2 4 1 2 5 5 2 6 9 0 8 2 9 1 6 3 4
    0 9 5 1 4 0 5 0 2 0 4 6 0 0 0 1 4 0 7 1 6
      1 6 9 0 1 7 9 9 7 9 0 1 9 5 9 0 1 4 5
        8 2 8 3 8 6 1 5 1 6 2 0 8 2 5 0 4
          7 1 6 2 1 1 9 7 4 2 0 4 7 1 6
            5 4 3 0 9 6 8 2 0 3 6 4 5
              6 7 3 6 4 6 6 7 6
                6 2 2 3 0 3 7
```

Serious Capture Board

```
                        3 6 4 7 2 3 6
                      0 3 4 3 1 6 1 3 6
                    3 0 7 5 1 6 8 2 3 1 2 3 0
                  7 1 6 6 7 3 2 4 6 0 2 5 7 1 6
                3 0 4 5 4 6 0 2 5 3 0 6 7 0 4 5 4 3 0
              7 1 6 5 0 3 6 9 9 5 7 7 0 5 5 5 0 3 7 1 6
              4 5 4 1 4 0 7 3 8 0 5 2 1 2 2 1 4 0 4 5 4
            3 0 5 0 3 9 0 1 5 4 9 5 6 2 0 5 6 9 0 1 5 0 3 3 0
          2 0 6 9 4 6 0 8 2 0 5 9 6 7 5 2 4 1 0 8 2 4 0 5 8 4 7
        1 4 2 1 7 1 4 8 8 5 6 2 5 0 8 8 1 0 4 6 1 8 2 5 6 2 1 7 2
        4 2 5 1 5 0 4 6 1 5 0 4 6 6 2 9 5 4 9 5 6 2 0 5 6 3 9 0 9
      7 9 7 3 9 6 9 7 4 0 5 5 4 5 9 4 0 5 9 6 7 5 2 4 1 5 3 9 6 4 7
      4 1 4 8 8 5 6 2 5 4 8 8 1 0 4 6 1 8 2 5 6 2 1 7 1 4 2 1 7 7 4
      5 2 3 0 9 7 2 3 1 6 4 6 1 1 7 4 6 1 7 4 7 1 6 1 0 6 0 9 7 1 5
      0 6 6 4 5 4 9 1 4 5 4 9 1 4 2 6 6 4 6 6 9 2 6 0 9 6 9 0 2 0 0
      6 3 6 4 7 2 3 6 1 5 3 5 7 3 9 1 5 0 9 6 5 0 3 7 6 5 4 7 2 7 6
      7 6 2 6 7 4 6 6 4 0 6 7 1 0 7 9 1 4 6 2 6 0 0 1 6 2 0 0 1 1 7
      9 4 7 1 5 0 4 7 0 8 1 3 2 1 5 0 8 6 5 7 4 6 5 2 8 3 1 5 0 2 9
      4 7 7 9 7 3 9 6 9 7 4 0 5 5 4 5 9 4 0 5 9 6 7 5 2 4 1 5 3 9 6
      4 1 4 8 8 5 6 2 5 0 8 8 1 0 4 6 1 8 2 5 6 2 1 7 1 4 2 1 7 7 4
      3 0 9 7 2 3 4 6 1 6 1 1 7 4 6 1 7 4 7 1 6 1 0 6 0 9 7 1 5 5 2
      0 6 6 4 5 4 9 1 4 5 4 9 1 4 2 6 6 4 5 6 9 2 6 0 9 6 9 0 2 0 0
      7 6 6 3 6 4 7 2 3 6 1 5 3 5 7 3 9 1 5 0 9 6 5 0 3 7 6 5 4 7 2
      7 6 2 6 7 4 6 6 4 0 6 7 1 0 7 9 1 4 6 2 6 0 0 1 6 2 0 0 1 1 7
      7 1 5 0 4 7 0 8 1 3 2 1 5 0 8 6 5 7 4 6 5 2 8 3 1 5 0 2 9 9 4
        3 6 0 8 7 2 5 2 8 7 2 5 2 1 6 4 0 3 4 3 1 6 1 3 6 2 1 9 1
        5 1 4 6 7 5 1 6 8 2 3 1 2 7 6 8 2 7 0 8 2 9 1 6 3 4 6 7 2
          6 1 4 0 9 5 1 4 0 6 0 2 5 3 0 6 7 0 1 4 0 7 1 6 2 7 3
            3 0 7 1 6 9 0 1 6 9 9 5 7 7 0 5 5 9 0 1 4 5 4 3 0
              4 5 4 0 8 2 7 3 8 0 5 2 1 2 2 0 8 2 5 0 3
              5 0 3 7 1 6 6 1 1 7 4 6 1 7 4 7 1 6 7 1 6
                3 0 4 5 4 6 0 9 6 9 0 2 6 6 4 5 4 3 0
                  5 0 3 5 7 3 9 1 5 0 9 6 5 0 3
                    3 0 1 6 2 6 7 4 5 6 4 3 0
                      0 6 4 7 2 1 1 7 5
                        3 6 4 7 2 3 6
```

CRYPTO GAME

Players: Any number.

Requirements:
Pencils and paper.
1 Calculator per player.

How it works

1. Players take turns to say any single digit number, including zero. That number is added to a total written on a sheet of paper between the players, until the required number of digits is reached.

2. The game is then to get four functions, +, −, ÷, x, to total the sum in the middle exactly.

3. Crypto is best played with a 3-digit number for younger players, a 4-digit number for teenagers, and a 5-digit number for adults.

4. Players can agree to upgrade or downgrade to a different level of play by adding or removing digits from the figure to get.

Rules

1. Two of the operations must be with double-digit numbers.
2. Each funtion must be used once only.
3. No number may be used more than once in each hand (2 and 22 are different numbers).
4. The first person to get five numbers which can be used with the four functions, to equal the solution, wins the hand. Winner shouts, "Crypto!"
5. The solution must be proved.
6. Players may work out the sum on paper, by calculator, or both.
7. The game is played in sets of five games per set, five sets per match.

Sample Game:

Player 1: "One."

Player 2: "Zero."

Player 3: "Zero."

Therefore, the target number here is 100.

Player 2:
"Crypto! 24 x 8 + 17 – 9 ÷ 2." (24 x 8) [192] + 17 – 9 [200] ÷ 2 = 100.

Player 1:
"You just beat me. I had 36 + 17 x 4 – 12 ÷ 2."
(36 + 17) [53] x 4 [212] – 12 [200] ÷ 2 =100.

Player 3:
"Beats me!"
Player 2 wins by getting the correct answer in first.

DOMINOES GAME

Players: 2 to 5

Requirements:

Domino number board.
Pencils and paper. **Player 1** is red; **Player 2** is blue, **Player 3** is green; **Player 4** is black; **Player 5** is brown, purple or orange. Calculators for kids under 8 optional.

How it works

1. Unlike ordinary dominoes, this game goes up to 9.
2. At the beginning of the game each player uses their pencil to outline a block of 14 numbers in a 7 x 2 grid. Those are the numbers that will be used for the game.
3. Toss a coin to see who goes first.
4. Each player in turn, starting anywhere on the board, draws a line through two numbers, (a Domino) choosing numbers that, combined with that player's future anticipated moves will allow the player to lay out further Dominoes.
5. When the numbers have been crossed out, the player writes them (lays them) on the blank part of the Domino board (the table) on two consecutive squares.
6. Just like real dominoes, after the first two numbers have been laid on the table, other Dominoes may be laid at either end of the original Domino.
7. Each player tries to block the others from laying Dominoes, by choosing numbers that the other players will not be able to match.
8. Players may cover their selection of numbers with a sheet of paper, to stop other players seeing them.
9. Only numbers that lie at 90° to the selected grid can be used as Dominoes, as in the numbers selected below. Player 1 has chosen the horizontal grid. Player 2 has chosen the vertical grid.
10. Player 1 has played 3:7, Player 2 has played 7:8, Player 1 has played 8:6. Player 2 cannot play to the 6 – there are no 6s in their set – and so must play the 3:2. Player 1 now has the option of playing a 2:3 or a 2:5, and so on.

9	4	9	5	3	3	8	2	2	7	3							
2	8	3	1	5	0	4	7	1	5	0							
0	5	9	6	1	5	6	2	2	4	0							
9	1	2	1	6	0	5	3	4	9	0					3	7	7
3	9	7	8	0	2	2	7	7	8	1							8
7	9	0	6	8	5	3	3	4	1	2							8
2	1	6	8	4	1	0	5	3	2	0							6
4	7	3	6	4	8	0	3	5	4	6							
5	1	2	7	0	8	6	2	2	8	7							
7	2	0	1	7	7	9	8	7	4	9							
5	0	3	7	6	5	4	7	2	8	6							

11. The object is to achieve lay all your Dominoes out and make the other players clap. (See rules)

12. When neither player can make a move, the player with the least total value of dominoes left wins the game.

13. If both players are left with the same total value, the player with the least number of dominoes left wins.

Rules

1. When a player cannot go the player must pass, by knocking the board with the words, "I am clapping."

2. Only vertical and horizontals can be played. You cannot lay a Domino diagonally.

3. When a player cannot move during a game that player may begin a new line, but all moves from the old line are lost.

4. When the board is full, so that a new game cannot begin, total claims are added up to see who wins the set.

Minor Domino Boards

2	4	9	1	5	3	8	7	2	5	0
0	8	3	6	1	0	4	2	1	4	0
9	5	9	1	6	5	6	3	2	9	0
3	1	2	8	0	0	5	7	4	8	1
7	9	7	6	8	2	2	3	7	1	2
2	9	0	8	4	5	3	5	4	2	0
4	1	6	6	4	1	0	3	3	4	6
5	7	3	7	0	8	0	2	5	8	7
7	1	2	1	7	8	6	8	2	4	9
5	2	0	7	6	7	9	7	7	8	6
9	0	3	5	3	5	4	2	2	7	3

Major Domino Board

4	5	4	6	1	6	1	3	7	4	3	0	9	5	6	0	0	7	0	6	0	4
2	0	4	0	7	4	7	7	0	9	6	9	8	5	3	7	1	5	0	2	0	6
2	1	9	0	7	7	0	8	6	7	6	3	1	0	7	2	1	2	5	4	1	5
1	3	1	9	6	2	3	4	9	1	7	1	9	7	5	6	2	7	2	7	5	6
3	4	0	6	2	4	3	6	5	2	6	0	3	6	4	0	0	6	4	4	0	4
6	6	2	7	0	3	6	1	0	3	6	7	2	9	9	5	6	9	6	5	6	3
0	2	4	0	7	1	6	2	1	0	5	6	4	6	1	4	1	6	6	0	1	7
5	5	6	2	9	0	6	2	4	4	1	6	4	7	7	1	5	7	4	6	1	6
4	7	8	1	2	7	5	7	5	2	0	5	3	6	2	5	5	7	5	7	5	1
5	5	2	7	7	4	7	3	8	3	1	3	2	9	5	7	2	9	7	9	2	3
9	1	2	6	3	5	5	6	2	2	2	1	2	7	3	8	6	7	4	8	1	9

Serious Domino Board

7	0	6	5	2	4	6
5	8	2	7	0	1	1
0	9	6	3	2	5	2
2	6	7	1	5	0	5
8	4	6	5	6	8	1
1	6	4	7	0	6	6
0	2	6	9	6	4	6
5	.	3	6	5	6	6
7	1	4	7	9	2	3
1	6	5	6	0	4	1
5	5	6	5	7	4	1
3	4	9	8	9	7	5
5	7	4	8	3	8	6
1	9	6	2	6	1	6
2	9	0	8	6	4	8
6	0	6	5	3	0	2
7	0	6	5	2	4	3
8	2	7	0	1	9	5
0	9	6	3	2	2	2
2	6	7	1	9	0	5
8	4	6	5	5	8	1
1	6	4	7	0	5	6
0	2	6	9	6	1	6
5	0	3	6	5	6	6
7	1	4	7	9	2	3
1	6	5	6	0	4	1
5	5	6	5	7	4	1
3	4	9	8	9	7	5
5	7	4	8	3	8	6
1	9	6	2	6	1	6
2	9	0	8	6	4	8
6	0	6	5	3	0	2
7	0	6	5	2	4	3
8	2	7	0	1	9	5
0	9	6	3	2	2	2
2	6	7	1	9	0	5
8	4	6	5	5	8	1

KNIGHT NUMBERS GAMES

Players: 2 – 4

Requirements:
Knight Numbers board.
Pencils and paper. **Player 1** is red; **Player 2** is blue; **Player 3** is green; **Player 4** is black.
Calculators are optional.

How it works

1. The object is to achieve the highest score at the end of the game, when all the numbers each player has crossed through are added together to give a final total.

Sample game

Player chooses 6–9–9–8.

2	7	0	6	2
2	3	6	9	4
3	1	8	9	3
8	3	6	8	6
1	2	5	4	3

Player 2 does the same, choosing numbers that are as high as possible and which may help to block the other players from getting a good score. The nunbers chosen are 8–6–5–4.

2	7	0	6	2
2	3	6	9	4
3	1	8	9	3
8	3	6	8	6
1	2	5	4	3

Rules

No square may be visited more than once. Other players' lines cannot be crossed. Each line has to be shaped like an 'L', three numbers in one direction, then one at a right angle. The game is over when no more lines of four numbers can be made. All the numbers each player has drawn a line through are added together, and whoever has the biggest total wins.

Minor Knight Number Boards

7	1	8	9	2	6	7	0
0	2	7	6	3	1	1	9
9	5	5	5	7	8	6	2
3	1	0	2	3	6	0	7
7	9	2	3	5	8	8	0
2	9	5	0	3	6	4	6
4	1	1	0	2	7	4	3
5	7	8	6	8	1	0	2

Major Knight Number Board

2	4	9	7	1	5	4	1	7	5	5	6	5	7	7	1
3	9	3	5	7	4	3	2	2	5	3	4	9	8	3	7
2	7	4	5	1	0	7	8	0	1	6	5	6	0	6	2
1	9	3	6	5	3	2	4	5	0	3	6	5	6	7	7
6	0	4	2	7	6	1	0	6	1	4	7	9	2	6	0
4	9	5	7	0	9	6	3	5	5	2	6	7	1	4	9
8	0	5	4	8	1	7	2	6	1	8	4	6	5	2	1
4	2	3	5	6	9	0	1	6	0	6	5	3	0	7	4
6	7	2	1	8	5	7	4	3	2	9	0	8	6	1	6
7	5	9	0	7	4	1	9	6	0	6	5	2	4	9	0
0	4	2	8	5	3	7	0	1	8	2	7	0	1	2	7
6	5	9	6	2	4	0	1	5	0	9	6	3	2	4	5
4	7	1	3	6	2	7	0	6	1	6	4	7	0	1	9
2	9	6	4	6	1	9	5	4	0	2	6	9	6	6	4
0	5	1	7	8	4	0	1	3	6	5	7	4	8	2	5
1	3	4	2	6	5	2	8	0	1	9	6	2	6	3	7

Serious Knight Number Board

```
3 6 4 7 2 3 6 1 5 3 5 7 3 9 1 5 0 9 6 5 0 3 7 6 5 4 7 2
6 2 6 0 0 1 6 2 0 0 1 6 2 8 7 4 6 6 4 0 6 7 1 0 7 9 1 4
0 5 8 2 7 0 5 2 1 4 0 6 4 7 2 1 1 7 5 6 1 6 6 0 0 8 2 7
5 7 2 1 9 7 7 9 4 2 1 5 4 6 5 5 5 7 7 7 1 1 4 5 7 1 1 4
4 5 2 7 3 4 5 3 7 3 2 3 3 9 3 7 5 9 4 9 5 3 3 8 2 2 7 3
2 8 3 1 5 0 4 7 1 5 0 4 7 0 8 1 3 2 1 5 0 8 6 5 7 4 6 5
5 2 8 7 2 5 2 1 6 4 0 3 4 3 1 6 1 3 6 2 1 9 3 6 0 8 7 2
5 1 6 8 2 3 1 2 7 6 8 2 7 0 8 2 9 1 6 3 4 6 7 5 1 4 6 7
0 5 8 2 7 0 5 2 1 4 0 6 4 7 2 1 1 7 5 6 1 6 6 0 0 8 2 7
4 5 2 7 3 4 5 3 7 3 2 3 3 9 3 7 5 9 4 9 5 3 3 8 2 2 7 3
4 7 0 8 1 3 2 1 5 0 8 6 5 7 4 6 5 2 8 3 1 5 0 4 7 1 5 0
5 2 8 7 2 5 2 1 6 4 0 3 4 3 1 6 1 3 6 2 1 9 3 6 0 8 7 2
1 6 3 4 6 7 5 1 4 6 7 5 1 6 8 2 3 1 2 7 6 8 2 7 0 8 2 9
9 5 1 4 0 9 5 4 6 3 6 7 3 2 4 6 0 2 5 3 0 6 7 0 6 1 4 0
9 5 4 6 3 6 7 3 2 4 6 0 2 5 3 0 6 7 0 6 1 4 0 9 5 1 4 0
4 0 9 0 1 4 0 7 7 9 6 9 9 5 7 7 0 5 5 2 0 6 9 4 6 9 0 1
2 1 1 0 7 7 3 8 0 7 7 3 8 0 5 2 1 2 2 4 0 5 8 4 7 0 8 2
4 6 1 5 0 4 6 6 2 9 5 4 9 5 6 2 0 5 6 3 0 9 4 2 5 1 5 0
9 7 4 0 5 5 4 5 9 4 0 5 9 6 7 5 2 4 1 5 3 9 6 9 7 3 9 6
1 4 2 1 7 1 4 8 8 5 6 2 5 0 8 8 1 0 4 6 1 8 2 5 6 2 1 7
4 2 5 1 5 0 4 6 1 5 0 4 6 6 2 9 5 4 9 5 6 2 0 5 6 3 0 9
9 7 3 9 6 9 7 4 0 5 5 4 5 9 4 0 5 9 6 7 5 2 4 1 5 3 9 6
1 4 8 8 5 6 2 5 0 8 8 1 0 4 6 1 8 2 5 6 2 1 7 1 4 2 1 7
2 3 0 9 7 2 3 4 6 1 6 1 1 7 4 6 1 7 4 7 1 6 1 0 6 0 9 7
6 6 4 5 4 9 1 4 5 4 9 1 4 2 6 6 4 6 6 9 2 6 0 9 6 9 0 2
3 6 4 7 2 3 6 1 5 3 5 7 3 9 1 5 0 9 6 5 0 3 7 6 5 4 7 2
6 2 6 7 4 6 6 4 0 6 7 1 0 7 9 1 4 6 2 6 0 0 1 6 2 0 0 1
4 7 1 5 0 4 7 0 8 1 3 2 1 5 0 8 6 5 7 4 6 5 2 8 3 1 5 0
3 6 0 8 7 2 5 2 8 7 2 5 2 1 6 4 0 3 4 3 1 6 1 3 6 2 1 9
5 1 4 6 7 5 1 6 8 2 3 1 2 7 6 8 2 7 0 8 2 9 1 6 3 4 6 7
9 5 4 6 3 6 7 3 2 4 6 0 2 5 3 0 6 7 0 6 1 4 0 9 5 1 4 0
4 0 9 0 1 4 0 7 7 9 6 9 9 5 7 7 0 5 5 2 0 6 9 4 6 9 0 1
2 1 1 0 7 7 3 8 0 7 7 3 8 0 5 2 1 2 2 4 0 5 8 4 7 0 8 2
2 3 0 9 7 2 3 4 6 1 6 1 1 7 4 6 1 7 4 7 1 6 1 0 6 0 9 7
1 4 2 6 6 4 6 6 9 2 6 0 9 6 9 0 2 6 6 4 5 4 9 1 4 5 4 9
3 6 4 7 2 3 6 1 5 3 5 7 3 9 1 5 0 9 6 5 0 3 7 6 5 4 7 2
6 2 6 0 0 1 6 2 0 0 1 6 2 6 7 4 6 6 4 0 6 7 1 0 7 9 1 4
0 5 8 2 7 0 5 2 1 4 0 6 4 7 2 1 1 7 5 6 1 6 6 0 0 8 2 7
5 7 2 1 9 7 7 9 4 2 1 5 4 6 5 5 5 7 7 7 1 1 4 5 7 1 1 4
4 5 2 7 3 4 5 3 7 3 2 3 3 9 3 7 5 9 4 9 5 3 3 8 2 2 7 3
```

NOUGHTS AND CROSSES

Using **4096** as a base

Players: 2

Requirements:
Pencils and paper.
Calculator.

How it Works

1. There are two main games; 5-straight, and 4-square.

2. The object of the 5-straight game is to make a line of five noughts or crosses, horizontally, vertically or diagonally.

3. The object of the 4-square game is to game is to make a 2 x 2 square of noughts or crosses.

4. Toss a coin to decide who goes first. The person going first writes a cross.

5. Enter 4096 into the calculator.

6. Player 1 divides that by any number between 64 and 2049 – e.g. 66. Result = 62.0606r.

7. Numbers after the decimal point are ignored, so Player 1 marks square 62 with a cross.

8. Player 2 then repeats the process using a different divisor.

Rules

1. The play mode must be agreed before play begins: Either 5-straight or 4-square.

2. If a divisor produces a result that has already been used, the player gets to try again.

3. The winner is the first to get 5-straight or 4-square, according to the game being played.

4. The winner can choose whether to abandon the board or play on to try to get another line or block on the same board. Players can agree to switch between play modes.

Sample games:

1	2	3	4	5	6	7	8
9	10	11	12	13	14	15	16
17	18	19	20	21	22	23	24
25	26	27	28	29	30	31	32
33	34	35	36	37	38	39	40
41	42	43	44	45	46	47	48
49	50	51	52	53	54	55	56
57	58	59	60	61	62	63	64

1	2	3	4	5	6	7	8
9	10	11	12	13	14	15	16
17	18	19	20	21	22	23	24
25	26	27	28	29	30	31	32
33	34	35	36	37	38	39	40
41	42	43	44	45	46	47	48
49	50	51	62	53	54	55	56
57	58	59	60	61	62	63	64

5-straight — Player 1 wins.   **4-square — Player 2 wins.**

Noughts and Crosses Game Boards

1	2	3	4	5	6	7	8
9	10	11	12	13	14	15	16
17	18	19	20	21	22	23	24
25	26	27	28	29	30	31	32
33	34	35	36	37	38	39	40
41	42	43	44	45	46	47	48
49	50	51	52	53	54	55	56
57	58	59	60	61	62	63	64

1	2	3	4	5	6	7	8
9	10	11	12	13	14	15	16
17	18	19	20	21	22	23	24
25	26	27	28	29	30	31	32
33	34	35	36	37	38	39	40
41	42	43	44	45	46	47	48
49	50	51	52	53	54	55	56
57	58	59	60	61	62	63	64

1	2	3	4	5	6	7	8
9	10	11	12	13	14	15	16
17	18	19	20	21	22	23	24
25	26	27	28	29	30	31	32
33	34	35	36	37	38	39	40
41	42	43	44	45	46	47	48
49	50	51	52	53	54	55	56
57	58	59	60	61	62	63	64

1	2	3	4	5	6	7	8
9	10	11	12	13	14	15	16
17	18	19	20	21	22	23	24
25	26	27	28	29	30	31	32
33	34	35	36	37	38	39	40
41	42	43	44	45	46	47	48
49	50	51	52	53	54	55	56
57	58	59	60	61	62	63	64

1	2	3	4	5	6	7	8
9	10	11	12	13	14	15	16
17	18	19	20	21	22	23	24
25	26	27	28	29	30	31	32
33	34	35	36	37	38	39	40
41	42	43	44	45	46	47	48
49	50	51	52	53	54	55	56
57	58	59	60	61	62	63	64

1	2	3	4	5	6	7	8
9	10	11	12	13	14	15	16
17	18	19	20	21	22	23	24
25	26	27	28	29	30	31	32
33	34	35	36	37	38	39	40
41	42	43	44	45	46	47	48
49	50	51	52	53	54	55	56
57	58	59	60	61	62	63	64

1	2	3	4	5	6	7	8
9	10	11	12	13	14	15	16
17	18	19	20	21	22	23	24
25	26	27	28	29	30	31	32
33	34	35	36	37	38	39	40
41	42	43	44	45	46	47	48
49	50	51	52	53	54	55	56
57	58	59	60	61	62	63	64

1	2	3	4	5	6	7	8
9	10	11	12	13	14	15	16
17	18	19	20	21	22	23	24
25	26	27	28	29	30	31	32
33	34	35	36	37	38	39	40
41	42	43	44	45	46	47	48
49	50	51	52	53	54	55	56
57	58	59	60	61	62	63	64

1	2	3	4	5	6	7	8
9	10	11	12	13	14	15	16
17	18	19	20	21	22	23	24
25	26	27	28	29	30	31	32
33	34	35	36	37	38	39	40
41	42	43	44	45	46	47	48
49	50	51	52	53	54	55	56
57	58	59	60	61	62	63	64

1	2	3	4	5	6	7	8
9	10	11	12	13	14	15	16
17	18	19	20	21	22	23	24
25	26	27	28	29	30	31	32
33	34	35	36	37	38	39	40
41	42	43	44	45	46	47	48
49	50	51	52	53	54	55	56
57	58	59	60	61	62	63	64

1	2	3	4	5	6	7	8
9	10	11	12	13	14	15	16
17	18	19	20	21	22	23	24
25	26	27	28	29	30	31	32
33	34	35	36	37	38	39	40
41	42	43	44	45	46	47	48
49	50	51	52	53	54	55	56
57	58	59	60	61	62	63	64

1	2	3	4	5	6	7	8
9	10	11	12	13	14	15	16
17	18	19	20	21	22	23	24
25	26	27	28	29	30	31	32
33	34	35	36	37	38	39	40
41	42	43	44	45	46	47	48
49	50	51	52	53	54	55	56
57	58	59	60	61	62	63	64

PONTOONS GAME

Players: 2–4

Requirements:

Pontoons number board.

Pencils and paper. **Player 1** is red; **Player 2** is blue, **Player 3** is green; **Player 4** is black.

Calculators for kids under 8 (optional).

How it works

1. The object is to achieve 21 by linking numbers totalling 21.

```
2 7 0 6 2
2 3 6 9 4
3 1 5 9 3
8 3 6 8 6
1 2 5 4 3
```

Here a player has gone 2–3–5–6–5 and claimed "Pontoon"; the other player is not shown.

Rules

1. Players take it in turns to draw a line through one number.

2. A player cannot link on to another's line and claim Pontoon, or cross another player's line.

3. Each game can use either diagonal or horizontal and vertical lines, but not both.

4. If a player cannot move, or chooses not to move, their line ends at that point and is worth the numbers it contains.

5. A line that totals more than 21 points, known as going bust, is worth 0.

6. If neither player gets 21, whoever is closer to 21 without going bust is the winner of that round. If they get the same, the round is a draw.

7. When the board is full, whoever won more rounds wins the game.

Minor Pontoon Board

7	1	0	6	7	8	9	2
0	2	9	1	1	7	6	3
9	5	2	8	6	5	5	7
3	1	7	6	0	0	2	3
7	9	0	8	8	2	3	5
2	9	6	6	4	5	0	3
4	1	3	7	4	1	0	2
5	7	2	1	0	8	6	8

Major Pontoon Board

6	5	7	7	1	1	4	5	7	9	4	2	1	5	5
4	9	8	2	3	2	7	3	4	5	3	9	3	7	5	3
5	6	0	0	6	8	2	7	0	5	4	7	2	1	1	6
6	5	6	5	7	4	7	2	3	6	3	9	1	5	0	3
7	9	2	6	6	0	0	1	6	2	4	0	6	7	1	4
6	7	1	5	4	3	9	6	9	7	5	9	4	0	5	2
4	6	5	6	2	2	1	7	1	4	5	0	8	8	1	8
5	3	0	6	7	1	4	0	9	5	3	2	4	6	0	6
0	8	6	3	1	4	6	7	5	1	2	7	6	8	2	9
5	2	4	6	9	9	0	1	4	0	9	5	7	7	0	6
7	0	1	1	2	0	7	7	3	8	2	4	0	5	8	2
6	3	2	5	4	1	5	0	4	6	9	5	6	2	0	9
4	7	0	6	1	0	9	7	2	3	1	7	4	6	1	6
6	9	6	4	6	5	4	9	1	4	6	9	2	6	0	2
7	4	8	3	2	1	5	0	4	7	1	5	0	8	6	5
6	2	6	0	3	8	7	2	5	2	4	3	1	6	1	9

Serious Pontoon Board

```
5 7 3 9 1 5 0 4 7 2 3 6 1 5 3 9 6 5 0 3 7 6 5 4 7 2 3 6
6 6 4 0 6 7 1 0 0 1 6 2 6 7 4 0 7 9 1 4 6 2 6 0 0 1 8 2
0 6 4 7 2 1 1 8 2 7 0 5 2 1 4 7 5 6 1 6 6 0 0 8 2 7 0 5
7 7 9 4 2 1 5 1 1 5 4 7 2 1 9 4 6 5 5 5 7 7 7 1 1 4 5 7
2 3 3 9 3 7 5 2 7 3 4 5 3 7 3 9 4 9 5 3 3 8 2 2 7 3 4 5
3 2 1 5 0 8 6 1 5 0 4 7 0 8 1 5 7 4 6 5 2 8 3 1 5 0 4 7
0 3 4 3 1 6 1 8 7 2 5 2 1 6 4 3 6 2 1 9 3 6 0 8 7 2 5 2
3 1 2 7 6 8 2 4 6 7 5 1 6 8 2 7 0 8 2 9 1 6 3 4 6 7 5 1
6 7 3 2 4 6 0 1 4 0 9 5 4 6 3 2 5 3 0 6 7 0 6 1 4 0 9 5
6 9 9 5 7 7 0 9 0 1 4 0 7 7 9 5 5 2 0 6 9 4 6 9 0 1 4 0
1 2 2 4 0 5 8 0 7 7 3 8 0 5 2 4 7 0 8 2 2 1 1 0 7 7 3 8
5 4 9 5 6 2 0 1 5 0 4 6 6 2 9 5 6 3 0 9 4 2 5 1 5 0 4 6
5 4 5 9 4 0 5 3 9 6 9 7 4 0 5 9 6 7 5 2 4 1 5 3 9 6 9 7
6 2 5 0 8 8 1 2 1 7 1 4 8 8 5 0 4 6 1 8 2 5 6 2 1 4 1 4
8 1 1 7 4 6 1 0 9 7 2 3 4 6 1 7 4 7 1 6 1 0 6 0 9 7 2 3
4 6 6 9 2 6 0 5 4 9 1 4 2 6 6 9 6 9 0 2 6 6 4 5 4 9 1 4
5 7 3 9 1 5 0 4 7 2 3 6 1 5 3 9 6 5 0 3 7 6 5 4 7 2 3 6
6 6 4 0 6 7 1 0 0 1 6 2 6 7 4 0 7 9 1 4 6 2 6 0 0 1 6 2
0 6 4 7 2 1 1 8 2 7 0 5 2 1 4 7 5 6 1 6 6 0 0 8 2 7 0 5
7 7 9 4 2 1 5 1 1 4 5 7 2 1 9 4 6 5 5 5 7 7 7 1 1 4 5 7
2 3 3 9 3 7 5 2 7 3 4 5 3 7 3 9 4 9 5 3 3 8 2 2 7 3 4 5
3 2 1 5 0 8 6 1 5 0 4 7 0 8 1 5 7 4 6 5 2 8 3 1 5 0 4 7
0 3 4 3 1 6 1 8 7 2 5 2 1 6 4 3 6 2 1 9 3 6 0 8 7 2 5 2
3 1 2 7 6 8 2 4 6 7 5 1 6 8 2 7 0 8 2 9 1 6 3 4 6 7 5 1
6 7 3 2 4 6 0 1 4 0 9 5 4 6 3 2 5 3 0 6 7 0 6 1 4 0 9 5
6 9 9 5 7 7 0 9 0 1 4 0 7 7 9 5 5 2 0 6 9 4 6 9 0 1 4 0
1 2 2 4 0 5 8 0 7 7 3 8 0 5 2 4 7 0 8 2 2 1 1 0 7 7 3 8
5 4 9 5 6 2 0 1 5 0 4 6 6 2 9 5 6 3 0 9 4 2 5 1 5 0 4 6
5 4 5 9 4 0 5 3 9 6 9 7 4 0 5 9 6 7 5 2 4 1 5 3 9 6 9 7
6 2 5 0 8 8 1 2 1 7 1 4 8 8 5 0 4 6 1 8 2 5 6 2 1 7 1 4
3 6 4 7 2 3 6 1 5 3 5 7 3 9 1 5 0 9 6 5 0 3 7 6 5 4 7 2
6 1 1 7 4 6 1 0 9 7 2 3 4 6 1 7 4 7 1 6 1 0 6 0 9 7 2 3
4 6 6 9 2 6 0 5 4 9 1 4 2 6 6 9 6 9 0 2 6 6 4 5 4 9 1 4
5 7 3 9 1 5 0 4 7 2 3 6 1 5 3 9 6 5 0 3 7 6 5 4 7 2 3 6
6 6 4 0 6 7 1 0 0 1 6 2 6 7 4 0 7 9 1 4 6 2 6 0 0 1 6 2
0 6 4 7 2 1 1 8 2 7 0 5 2 1 4 7 5 6 1 6 6 0 0 8 2 7 0 5
7 7 9 4 2 1 5 1 1 4 5 7 2 1 9 4 6 5 5 5 7 7 7 1 1 4 5 7
2 3 3 9 3 7 5 2 7 3 4 5 3 7 3 9 4 9 5 3 3 8 2 2 7 3 4 5
3 2 1 5 0 8 6 1 5 0 4 7 0 8 1 5 7 4 6 5 2 8 3 1 5 0 4 7
0 3 4 3 1 6 1 8 7 2 5 2 1 6 4 3 6 2 1 9 3 6 0 8 7 2 5 2
3 1 2 7 6 8 2 4 6 7 5 1 6 8 2 7 0 8 2 9 1 6 3 4 6 7 5 1
6 7 3 2 4 6 0 1 4 0 9 5 4 6 3 2 5 3 0 6 7 0 6 1 4 0 9 5
```

RESPOND GAME

Players: 2

Requirements:
Respond board.
Pencils and paper. **Player 1** is red, **Player 2** is blue
Calculators permitted for under 12s.
Stopwatch or somebody to count to 10.

How it works

1. Flip a coin to choose who goes first.
2. Player 1 circles a number and says, "Respond!"
3. Player 2 has to Respond by adding, subtracting, multiplying or dividing numbers to get the circled number. On the Minor Board Player 2 then gets 10 seconds to Respond by selecting two numbers that can be combined; on the Major and Serious Boards, the players have 1 minute to Respond, but must use three numbers. In all games, the numbers are scored through.
4. The positions then reverse; Player 2 circles a number and Player 1 Responds as before.

Sample Game

Here Player 1 has challenged by circling 36, and Player 2 has responded by saying, "4 x 9".

Rules

1. Numbers may be used only once.

2. If a player cannot respond or runs out of time, the other player scores a point and gets to go first again.

3. At the end of the game, the player with most points wins.

Minor Respond Board

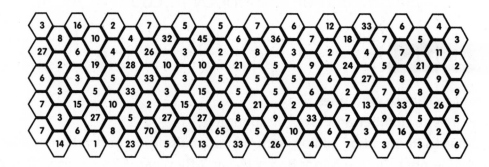

Major Respond Board

Serious Respond Board

TRACKER GAME

Players: 2 - 4

Requirements:
Tracker number board.

Pencils and paper. **Player 1** is red; **Player 2** is blue; **Player 3** is green; **Player 4** is black.

Calculators optional, but may only be used at the end when adding up Tracks.

How it works

1. The object is to achieve the highest score possible.

2. Toss a coin to see who goes first.

3. Each player in turn, starting anywhere on the board, draws a line through one number, choosing the highest potential Tracker line.

4. Tracker can be played with other numbers on the board.

Sample Game

Here one player has chosen to block one end of another player's route with the numbers 7–0–2–9–4.

```
3 7 0 2 9
2 3 7 9 4
7 1 5 9 3
8 3 8 8 6
0 2 5 4 8
```

Rules

1. Players move through one number each turn.

2. You cannot link on to another player's track, but may go off at 90° to a players last move, on the next square.

3. Except for squares with zero in them, other player's Tracks cannot be crossed. Crossing a zero counts as an ordinary move.

4. Diagonals OR vertical & horizontals can be played, but you cannot mix both in a game.

5. End changing is permitted. You may go back to your start square to change direction.

6. No backtracking on squares already taken.

7. This is a game of strategy. Blocking another player is permitted.

8. No middle track moves. You must continue from either end of your track.

9. When one player cannot move from either end of a track, the player who can still move wins that game, irrespective of the scores achieved.

10. When both players cannot move, the player who has the highest total wins that game.

11. Games are played until the board can take no more games.

12. When the board is full, the player with the highest total number of games wins the set.

Minor Tracker Board

0	2	3	8	9	2	7	1
2	3	5	7	6	3	0	2
5	0	3	5	5	7	9	5
4	1	6	0	6	7	3	1
5	7	8	8	1	1	7	9
2	0	6	4	8	6	2	9
7	9	3	7	4	1	0	2
0	6	2	1	0	8	6	8

Major Tracker Board

6	9	9	5	7	7	0	9	0	1	4	0	7	7	9	5
2	2	4	0	5	8	0	7	7	3	8	0	5	2	4	1
9	5	6	2	0	1	5	0	4	6	6	2	9	5	5	4
4	5	9	4	0	5	3	9	6	9	7	4	0	5	9	5
6	2	5	0	8	8	1	2	1	7	1	4	8	8	5	0
1	1	7	4	6	1	0	9	7	2	3	4	6	1	7	6
6	9	2	6	0	5	4	9	1	4	2	6	6	9	4	6
2	9	7	0	6	5	2	4	2	0	4	5	8	0	3	6
3	1	9	5	8	2	7	0	1	9	6	5	1	4	7	5
6	0	2	0	9	6	3	2	5	4	9	6	2	9	7	4
7	0	5	2	6	7	1	5	8	0	3	1	9	6	4	2
2	4	8	1	8	4	6	5	1	4	7	4	6	2	6	9
3	3	9	6	1	6	4	7	0	6	2	9	4	2	7	4
0	5	6	0	2	6	9	6	3	1	9	9	2	4	4	1
3	4	6	0	1	0	5	9	7	5	3	3	9	6	4	1
6	7	4	2	7	4	1	3	2	0	4	1	0	5	4	2

Serious Tracker Board

```
6 6 0 4 2 2 0 6 8 7 7 3 5 1 1 3 0 7 4 9 2 5 1 9 5 5 1 3
7 2 7 0 1 1 5 2 1 0 4 6 7 6 1 4 7 6 9 0 2 7 5 0 6 9 5 4
3 0 2 8 7 7 4 5 2 2 3 0 5 2 7 4 2 6 3 7 3 1 5 7 4 6 5 6
7 7 5 1 7 4 3 7 4 1 2 5 6 2 5 9 5 7 3 4 1 1 0 4 6 5 0 5
6 8 6 2 0 3 6 5 0 7 1 4 2 3 7 3 6 3 4 9 6 7 1 9 7 9 1 3
6 8 0 1 2 0 0 7 8 5 7 4 5 0 1 1 0 2 4 5 2 8 1 5 5 4 1 5
7 6 7 8 1 2 5 2 1 7 4 5 7 1 1 4 7 3 9 3 2 6 5 3 6 2 5 9
3 6 2 4 7 7 4 1 2 6 3 5 5 6 7 2 2 1 3 7 3 8 5 7 4 8 5 9
2 0 3 8 5 7 4 5 1 2 0 0 7 2 8 4 3 6 1 7 0 1 6 7 7 6 6 6
3 7 0 1 7 4 5 7 8 1 2 5 2 2 6 9 0 7 4 4 1 1 1 4 6 5 1 5
1 8 3 2 6 3 5 5 4 7 7 4 1 3 8 3 3 3 2 9 6 7 2 9 0 9 2 3
6 8 0 1 2 0 0 7 8 5 7 4 5 0 1 1 0 2 4 5 2 8 1 5 5 4 1 5
7 6 7 8 1 2 5 2 1 7 4 5 7 1 1 4 7 3 9 3 2 6 5 3 6 2 5 9
3 6 2 4 7 7 4 1 2 6 3 5 5 6 7 2 2 1 3 7 3 8 5 7 4 8 5 9
2 0 3 1 5 0 4 5 1 4 0 9 7 4 8 3 3 7 1 2 0 6 6 2 7 3 6 6
3 0 0 1 7 0 5 5 8 4 2 9 2 4 6 3 0 7 4 2 1 6 1 2 6 3 1 6
1 4 3 9 6 1 5 0 4 0 7 4 1 7 8 9 3 9 2 5 6 7 2 5 0 2 2 6
7 1 6 0 4 7 9 8 1 7 0 3 5 0 6 2 6 2 3 4 4 5 0 4 5 0 0 2
7 2 6 1 4 0 9 6 1 5 0 4 5 6 6 9 6 4 3 5 4 2 0 5 5 3 0 9
9 1 6 3 0 6 4 7 9 9 1 9 0 4 7 5 6 4 9 9 7 0 0 9 5 7 0 2
2 5 1 2 7 7 3 4 0 1 7 1 8 8 5 5 1 2 2 0 0 8 8 0 7 6 8 8
4 2 5 1 5 0 4 6 1 5 0 4 6 6 2 9 5 4 9 5 6 2 0 5 6 3 0 9
4 1 5 3 9 6 9 7 3 9 6 9 7 4 0 5 5 4 5 9 4 0 5 9 6 7 5 2
3 5 6 2 1 7 1 4 2 1 7 1 4 8 8 5 6 2 5 0 8 8 1 0 4 6 1 8
4 0 5 0 5 7 4 3 1 9 0 2 6 4 2 1 5 1 9 7 6 6 0 7 6 7 0 6
4 6 5 5 9 9 9 4 3 4 6 1 7 2 0 6 5 6 5 9 4 6 5 9 6 9 5 2
2 6 6 4 1 2 1 6 2 7 7 3 4 1 8 3 6 7 5 9 8 5 1 9 4 5 1 3
1 2 6 0 9 1 2 2 0 0 7 6 3 6 6 4 6 6 1 0 4 7 1 0 4 9 1 4
6 8 4 1 4 0 1 7 5 5 9 4 4 0 6 1 4 2 6 5 2 8 0 5 6 4 0 5
7 6 5 8 7 2 3 2 4 7 2 5 6 1 5 4 5 3 3 1 6 0 3 6 2 0 9
6 6 6 4 0 7 6 1 0 6 1 5 2 6 7 2 6 1 4 7 6 8 1 7 7 8 1 9
2 0 3 1 5 0 4 5 1 4 0 9 7 4 8 3 3 7 1 2 0 6 6 2 7 3 6 6
3 4 0 9 7 1 5 0 8 0 2 4 2 7 6 9 0 9 4 5 1 7 1 5 6 2 1 6
1 1 3 0 6 7 5 8 4 7 7 3 1 0 8 2 3 2 2 4 6 5 2 4 0 0 2 2
7 0 6 0 4 7 9 3 1 9 0 2 5 4 6 1 6 1 3 7 4 6 0 7 5 7 0 6
9 6 6 5 0 9 4 4 9 4 1 1 0 2 7 6 6 6 9 9 7 6 0 9 5 9 0 2
2 6 1 4 7 2 3 6 0 7 7 3 8 1 5 3 1 7 2 9 0 5 8 9 7 5 8 3
1 2 6 0 9 1 2 2 0 0 7 6 3 6 6 4 6 6 1 0 4 7 1 0 4 9 1 4
6 0 4 8 4 7 1 5 5 2 9 0 4 2 6 4 4 6 6 7 2 1 0 7 6 6 0 6
7 7 5 1 7 4 3 7 4 1 2 5 6 2 5 9 5 7 3 4 1 1 0 4 6 5 0 5
6 8 6 2 0 3 6 5 0 7 1 4 2 3 7 3 6 3 4 9 6 7 1 9 7 9 1 3
```

TWO UP GAME

Players: 2 - 4

Requirements:
A pair of dice.
Pencils and paper.
Calculator optional, but speeds up the game.

How it Works

1. Roll the pair of dice twice and note the results in the table. (Avoids arguments later.)

2. The object of the game is to mentally calculate or guess the nearest two double-digit multiplicands that will produce the results obtained by rolling the dice. When you roll two dice, generally one will land closer to you than the other, so write down the closest result first with each roll.

Sample game

Roll one obtains 2 and 1, with 2 landing closer. Roll 2 obtains 5 and 6 with the 6 being closer. This means the target number is 2165.
Player 1 tries: 38 x 56 (2128); Player 2 tries: 48 x 45 (2160)

Both tries are checked with the calculator, if one is available. Player 2 wins, because 2160 is closer to the target of 2165 than Player 1's 2128. In the table it looks like this:

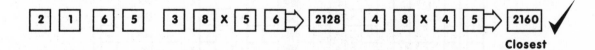

The winner, Player 2, then rolls the pair of dice again twice, and the set continues. Best out of 10 wins the round.

1. Players may not use multiples of 10, since it is a simple matter to divide any number in this way.

Two Up Tables

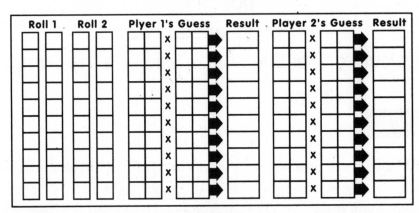

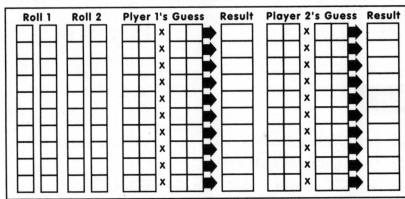

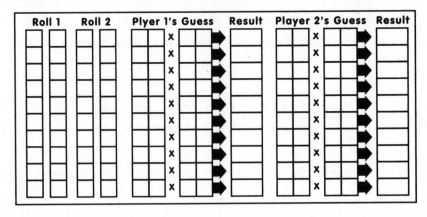

Two Up Tables

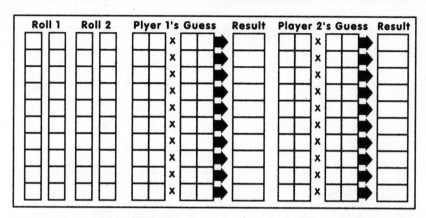

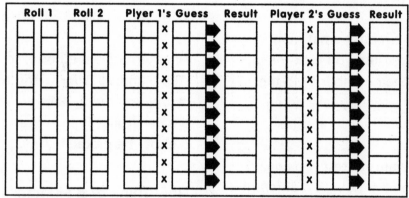

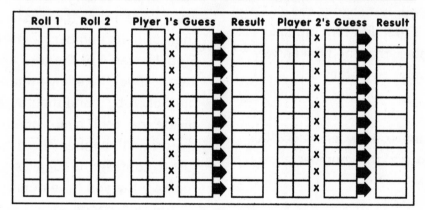

THINK OF A NUMBER

Try this with a friend. They'll think you are a real maths wizard:

1. Think of a number between 1 and 100 and take a note of that number.
2. Multiply it by 3
3. Add 45
4. Multiply by 2
5. Divide by 6
6. Subtract your original number
7. The answer is 15!

This trick works no matter what number you friend picks because you trick them into subtracting their number from the final result. What you are really doing is to change the final result to another number you know.

If your friend wants to test you again, you can do the same trick with a different number at the end. Just change the number in step 3 to a different multiple of 3 and remember that the final answer will be that number divided by 3.

For example:
1. Think of a number between 1 and 100 and take a note of that number.
2. Multiply it by 3
3. Add 75
4. Multiply by 2
5. Divide by 6
6. Subtract your original number
7. The answer is 25!

Or if you want to be very clever, you can choose a number for step 3 that doesn't divide evenly by 3. But this time, for the final answer you'll have to memorise whatever fraction you get as a result.

For example:
1. Think of a number between 1 and 100 and take a note of that number.
2. Multiply it by 3
3. Add 100
4. Multiply by 2
5. Divide by 6
6. Subtract your original number
7. The answer is 33.33 repeating for ever!

An alternative method is to leave off step 6 and ask your friend to tell you the result. You simply subtract your final answer from his answer and tell him the number he picked.

How Think of a Number tricks work

The real secret of the trick is subtracting their original number from the result. Step 2 x step 4 of the trick always equal step 5. If you take any number and multiply it by 3 and then by 2, and then divide the result by 6, you are left with the original number. The other steps are just to confuse the subjects so they won't realise what you have done.

You can change steps 2, 4 & 5 to be whatever you want, as long as step 2 x step 4 = step 5. The final answer will then always be step 3 / step 2.